Fuzzy Information Retrieval

Synthesis Lectures on Information Concepts, Retrieval, and Services

Editor
Gary Marchionini, *University of North Carolina, Chapel Hill*

Synthesis Lectures on Information Concepts, Retrieval, and Services publishes short books on topics pertaining to information science and applications of technology to information discovery, production, distribution, and management. Potential topics include: data models, indexing theory and algorithms, classification, information architecture, information economics, privacy and identity, scholarly communication, bibliometrics and webometrics, personal information management, human information behavior, digital libraries, archives and preservation, cultural informatics, information retrieval evaluation, data fusion, relevance feedback, recommendation systems, question answering, natural language processing for retrieval, text summarization, multimedia retrieval, multilingual retrieval, and exploratory search.

Fuzzy Information Retrieval
Donald H. Kraft and Erin Colvin

Incidental Exposure to Online News
Borchuluun Yadamsuren and Sanda Erdelez

Web Indicators for Research Evaluation: A Practical Guide
Michael Thelwall

Trustworthy Policies for Distributed Repositories
Hao Xu, Mike Conway, Arcot Rajasekar, Jon Crabtree, Helen Tibbo, and Reagan W. Moore

The Notion of Relevance in Information Science: Everybody knows what relevance is. But, what is it really?
Tefko Saracevic

Fuzzy Information Retrieval
Donald H. Kraft and Erin Colvin

ISBN: 978-3-031-01179-5 print
ISBN: 978-3-031-02307-1 ebook
DOI 10.1007/978-3-031-02307-1

A Publication in the Springer series
SYNTHESIS LECTURES ON INFORMATION CONCEPTS, RETRIEVAL, AND SERVICES #55

Series Editor: Gary Marchionini, University of North Carolina, Chapel Hill

Series ISSN 1947-945X Print 1947-9468 Electronic

Fuzzy Information Retrieval

Donald H. Kraft
Colorado Technical University and Louisiana State University
Erin Colvin
Western Washington University

*SYNTHESIS LECTURES ON INFORMATION CONCEPTS,
RETRIEVAL, AND SERVICES #55*

ABSTRACT

Information retrieval used to mean looking through thousands of strings of texts to find words or symbols that matched a user's query. Today, there are many models that help index and search more effectively so retrieval takes a lot less time. Information retrieval (IR) is often seen as a subfield of computer science and shares some modeling, applications, storage applications and techniques, as do other disciplines like artificial intelligence, database management, and parallel computing. This book introduces the topic of IR and how it differs from other computer science disciplines. A discussion of the history of modern IR is briefly presented, and the notation of IR as used in this book is defined. The complex notation of relevance is discussed. Some applications of IR is noted as well since IR has many practical uses today. Using information retrieval with fuzzy logic to search for software terms can help find software components and ultimately help increase the reuse of software. This is just one practical application of IR that is covered in this book.

Some of the classical models of IR is presented as a contrast to extending the Boolean model. This includes a brief mention of the source of weights for the various models. In a typical retrieval environment, answers are either yes or no, i.e., on or off. On the other hand, fuzzy logic can bring in a "degree of" match, vs. a crisp, i.e., strict match. This, too, is looked at and explored in much detail, showing how it can be applied to information retrieval. Fuzzy logic is often times considered a soft computing application and this book explores how IR with fuzzy logic and its membership functions as weights can help indexing, querying, and matching. Since fuzzy set theory and logic is explored in IR systems, the explanation of where the fuzz is ensues.

The concept of relevance feedback, including pseudorelevance feedback is explored for the various models of IR. For the extended Boolean model, the use of genetic algorithms for relevance feedback is delved into.

The concept of query expansion is explored using rough set theory. Various term relationships is modeled and presented, and the model extended for fuzzy retrieval. An example using the UMLS terms is also presented. The model is also extended for term relationships beyond synonyms.

Finally, this book looks at clustering, both crisp and fuzzy, to see how that can improve retrieval performance. An example is presented to illustrate the concepts.

KEYWORDS

information retrieval system (IRS), recall, precision, relevance, retrieval status value (RSV), ranking function, best match models (BM1), relevance feedback, mean average precision (MAP), TF-IDF, vector space model, probabilistic model, Boolean model

Contents

Preface

Where is the fuzz? Sounds like a silly question but is one that has plagued Erin in her short years in this field. She knows that this has been asked of her mentor, who co-authored this book. This may not be only a silly question but one that leads to a very open-ended dialog among computer and data scientists alike. To understand this topic, of "fuzzy logic" one must understand what the data is representing. We hope this book does a great job of explaining that while the data may be pointing to a solid Boolean explanation of yes/no, 1/0, on/off, as computer scientists like it, there are some gray areas that data scientists have found don't fit. That, is where the fuzz lays.

We all know how to search for anything we need on a computer, right? But a computer, being a simple Boolean machine, should know what you mean, when you mean jaguar the car, not the animal. This book is an exploration into different ways that algorithms can be set up to allow a weighted return of matches, maybe those that match your query return a higher number than those that don't and we form an increasing scale rather than a yes/no system. Or the feedback can be a continuous flow from user to search engine, constantly selecting only those matches that are positive and discarding those that are not. There are many ways searches can be altered to help users find a perfect match, the idea that a search result is not good/bad, yes/no, is where we find our "fuzzy" logic.

Acknowledgments

We would like to thank our families for their support and love. Erin would like to thank Gloria Bordogna and Gabriella Pasi for their continued support and ground-breaking work that allowed her to continue with her doctorate and this book.

CHAPTER 1

Introduction to Information Retrieval

1.1 DEFINING INFORMATION RETRIEVAL

There are many definitions of this relatively modern term. We start by recognizing that information retrieval (IR) is concerned with problems relating to the effective storage, access, and manipulation of primarily textual information. These are among the most interesting and challenging problems facing computer and information scientists. After all, information is continuing to grow in volume and is becoming increasingly available and accessible in computer formats. Moreover, computer networks and the Internet, as well as the World Wide Web, are making communication of information easier, while new computer architectures are making it more inexpensive. In addition, new technology, including artificial intelligence methods, has made feasible with the introduction of powerful and sophisticated algorithms to store, retrieve, and present massive volumes of information on a variety of media in new and better ways. Of course, issues such as cross-language retrieval, multimedia and hypertext/hypermedia, natural language processing, digital libraries, and web retrieval make retrieval even more interesting and challenging (Baeza-Yates and Ribeiro-Neto, 2011).

Permit us to paraphrase some of the other leading scholars in this IR discipline, including Robert Korfhage, Stephen Harter, and Gerard Salton (Salton et al., 1983). IR involves the location and presentation to a user of information relevant to an information need expressed as a query. An information retrieval system (IRS) is a device interposed between a potential user of information and the information collection itself; for a given information problem, the purpose of the system is to capture wanted items and to filter out unwanted items. After all, a good IR system should be able to extract meaningful (relevant) information while withholding non-relevant information. Moreover, IR deals with the representation, storage, and access to documents or representatives of documents (surrogates). We note that the term "document" may include text but it also may include non-print items such as images, animation, sounds, multimedia items, web pages, tweets, and blogs, among other possible pieces of information.

There are many elements within the concept of an information retrieval system. Figure 1.1 illustrates these elements, which include the selection of which documents to consider, and the acquisition of these items either as entire items or as pieces of metadata that describe them. Once the item, or the description of the item, is acquired, one must store it in a collection in some fashion. This concept of a description means indexing the items to determine such metadata. This could include bibliographic information such as title, author, publisher, publication date and the like (sometimes called descriptive cataloging for text documents). It can also include descriptions of the content of the item, e.g., keywords or index terms (sometimes called subject cataloging for text documents). Even non-print items can have descriptive metadata. For example, photographs can have written on the back or in the margins details such as the dates or the locations of the photographs. Of course, these descriptions must be stored. In addition, a document representation is inexact, i.e., ambiguous.

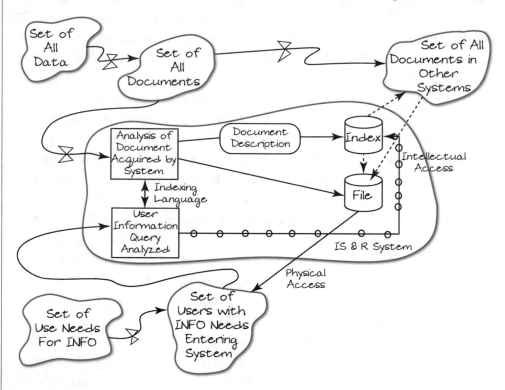

Figure 1.1: Model of information storage and retrieval system.

There is no reason to acquire and store information if it is never used. So, the next element in an information retrieval process is the ability to have a user who desires information able to express that need. Information problems causing the user to have a need and acting upon it can be modeled to include the visceral, i.e., a recognition of a deficiency of information although it may not be cognitively defined, so there is a gap or what some call an anomalous state of knowledge, i.e., a defect in the user's mental model. Then, there is the conscious, i.e., the user's characterization of this deficiency of information and the formalized, i.e., the user's clear articulation of this deficiency. Finally, there is the compromised level, where the formalized statement is limited by the search system. Problems arise in that the information need is amorphous, i.e., hard to express exactly.

Once the query is stated, the issue is to match the query to the collection of documents in order to retrieve the ones deemed relevant to the user's query while striving to avoid retrieval of those deemed not relevant. The actual act of retrieval can be seen as a matching of the terms in the document description to the terms in the query. This process of matching can be seen as being probabilistic rather than deterministic, unlike retrieval from a standard database management system. The reason for such difficulties is that the process is imprecise, that is, or otherwise described as vague and uncertain.

Then there is the output mechanism to tell the user what the results of the retrieval process have been. This is often seen as a list of the documents that the system deems as relevant to the user's query, often in ranked order. We note that the ability to allow the user to input queries and to get retrieval results requires a user interface mechanism.

There can be a feedback mechanism to allow the user to determine which of the retrieved documents are really relevant, or useful. It can also allow for modifications to the query to improve the results.

In addition, there may be links to other retrieval systems via what is sometimes called a union catalog. For example, libraries use this concept for inter-library loan activities. Moreover, there are meta-search engines that search various web search engines to help improve retrieval effectiveness.

In terms of retrieval tasks, they can be classified as being of two categories. One category is called ad hoc retrieval or retrospective retrieval. These tasks consist of looking at a relatively nonvolatile collection of documents and responding to user queries as they come to the IRS. On the other hand, the other category is called filtering or selective dissemination of information (SDI) or current awareness, and the IRS can be currently labeled as a recommender system. These tasks consist of looking at relatively static queries based on user profiles to alert users to new documents as they come to the IRS.

In terms of designing IRSs, there are two, often diametrically different, approaches. One is the system-centered approach, concentrating on computing issues and IR models, which is discussed later in this book. The alternative is the user-centered approach, dealing with issues having to do with the user as a person. The latter includes personalized and context-aware approaches.

1.1.1   RETRIEVAL METRICS

The evaluation of retrieval results is essential, especially in terms of determining whether a given retrieval system is an improvement over other systems. The usual measures are recall (Re), the proportion of relevant documents that are retrieved, and precision (Pn), the proportion of retrieved documents that are relevant. It is noteworthy that in the context of statistical decision theory, recall can be viewed as being equal to $1-\alpha$, where α is the Type I error (rejecting a relevant document); and precision can be viewed as being equal to $1-\beta$, where β is the Type II error (accepting a nonrelevant document). In statistics, the basis for decisions rest on the Neyman-Pearson lemma, which in this context implies finding the maximum precision subject to a constraint that recall is not less than $1-\alpha$. Also noteworthy is that recall is often difficult to measure and that precision is related to search length. Moreover, it is often the case that recall and precision are inversely related.

Combinations of the two measures are possible. One such combination is van Rijsbergen's E measure, which allows a user to specify importance of recall and precision: $E = 1 - 1/[\alpha Pn{\text -}1 + (1-\alpha Re{\text -}1)]$, where α is a user-specified parameter. We note that $\alpha > 1$ emphasizes precision, while $\alpha < 1$ emphasizes recall. A similar combination is the F measure: $F = (1+\alpha)*Pn*Re / (\alpha Pn + Re)$.

Another related measure, used in Colvin (2014), is Robertson's OKAPI BM25 measure (Robertson et al., 2004) and given as

$\Sigma term_j \in query\ IDF(j)*[f(j)*(k+1)]/[f(j)+k*factor]$,

where

- factor = $1-b+[b*|D|/avgdl]$,
- $IDF(j) = \log\{(N-ni+0.5\}/(ni+0.5)\}$,
- N = number of documents in collection,
- nj = number of documents with term j,
- f(j) = number of times term j is in document d,
- $|d|$ = number of words in document d (i.e., its length),
- avgdl = average length of documents in collection, and
- k and b are parameters (perhaps k=2.0 and b=0.75).

It has been suggested (Kraft, 1985) that the act of retrieval should be informative in terms of relevance, i.e., the probability of relevance given retrieval should exceed the probability of relevance. It terms of our performance measures, this is precision = Pn = Pr(relevance | retrieval) > generality = G = Pr(relevance), where Pr(.) implies a probability. We note that this is quite a weak rule, that the act of retrieval should yield a richer set of relevant documents that a random set taken from the collection.

Other related measures include generality (G), the proportion of the documents in the collection that are relevant, and fallout (Fa), the proportion of nonrelevant documents that are retrieved.

Recall and precision deal with a specific query and measuring the time and accuracy inside of one query's algorithm. But what if there are multiple search algorithms that need to be compared to each other, the measure most commonly used for that is a derivative of the recall and precision called the MAP, or mean average precision. This is calculated by taking the average recall and precision for all queries for a search and dividing by the number of queries run. This allows searches to be compared against each other if they use different IRSs.

Recall and precision are related to the effectiveness of the retrieval system. Other measures can be related to efficiency, including cost and time and effort to retrieve. One overall measure would be user satisfaction with the retrieval system. Clearly, these performance measures are essential to proper management of the information retrieval system.

1.2 A BIT OF IR HISTORY

First, one can consider libraries as IRSs, which they truly are. There are the ancient libraries such as the ones created by pioneers such as Ashurbanipal or the library at Alexandria in Egypt. Then, we have more modern libraries, no doubt influenced by technology, such as the printing press, the card catalog, classification systems such as the Dewey Decimal System or the Library of Congress system, the notion of key word in context (KWIC) indexing, union catalogs, and computers.

With the advent of the computer age came the notion of modeling of the IR process. We address some of these models later.

Some of the computing issues affecting information retrieval include the notion of data storage. Progress in data storage technology has seen the evolution from punched tape to punched cards to magnetic disk drives to floppy disk drives to CD and now to DVD drives. Related to storage is the ability to compress information, more specifically, the art of reducing the number of bits needed to store or transmit data. We note that compression can be lossy or lossless, the later implying that the compressed file can be decompressed to exactly its original value. Related to storage and transmission is the concept of security, keeping the ability to see or to modify data in the hands of only those who are allowed to do so. One method for keeping data confidential is encryption.

Modern computer architectures, including parallel and distributed architectures, allow for more efficient processing of data. Modern computer networking technologies allow for more efficient transmission of data. On the human side of the ledger, modern notions of user front ends, or user interfaces, allow for easier use of IRSs

In terms of computer algorithms, better means of finding data and file structures and the algorithms to manipulate them help retrieval performance. If one is dealing with primary key (unique identifier) search, we can consider retrieval via linear search or sorted file search with binary search or binary search trees, index sequential files, other tree search mechanisms (such as b-tree or b+ or b* trees), or even quad trees and tries, linked lists, or hash functions. For dealing with other data elements, we can consider indexes. Related to search is the notion of signature files, a bit-mapped abstraction related to hashing. In addition, one can consider indexing via n-grams, n letters (or even words) in a row from text.

Of course, modern retrieval systems often involve the use of search engines. These can be for web pages, e.g., Google or Yahoo, and the like. Metasearch engines have evolved that search several web search engines, e.g., Dogpile. It can be for text documents, such as Dialog or Medline, and the like. Also, some retrieval processes tend to use clustering, either storing or retrieving groups of documents that share some common characteristics.

Modern computing has allowed for great potential in retrieval. Going beyond text retrieval to dealing with non-print media is but one area. Dealing with cross-language retrieval with queries in one language but with documents in another language is a current topic of research. The use of artificial intelligence (AI), including natural language processing and summarization, has been controversial but has much potential as well. For example, research is ongoing into determining the emotion, or the opinions of the authors of political blogs. Computing has led the development of a variety of digital libraries.

In addition, today we have collaborative search engines that let users combine their IR activities, sharing information resources. We also have contextual search, where the IRS considers the full text of the user's query in order to determine the context of the request for information. Moreover, there is faceted search, dealing with a faceted classification mechanism to organize documents. Each facet corresponds to a specific characteristic of the document, and this corresponds to the more modern notion of frames in AI. Using IR to search big data is another opportunity for new research to help sort through the mass amounts of metadata that haven't even been scrubbed or indexed yet. This includes web search engines, given the vast numbers of web pages that are out there. Moreover, the use of modern analytics to analyze and interpret big data and to do data mining to develop new conclusions are being developed. There are many uses for a good, fast IRS, like finding software components for reuse that can save companies thousands of dollars in development time and time to market and many more (Kraft, 1985).

1.3   THE KEY NOTION OF RELEVANCE

The main objective of information retrieval systems is to present to the user a set of documents that are relevant to the user given his/her query. Researchers, especially those in the user-centered side of the discipline, have done extensive work on what relevance really is. Surely, it consists of a connection between a user, his/her need for information, the specific situation at hand, and the information itself. This includes issues of the user's goals and beliefs and knowledge at the time of the query because the relevance of a document is in the eye of the beholder, or in this case, the user.

The systems-centered researchers, and practitioners for that matter, have concentrated on relevance in terms of topicality or pertinence or "aboutness." Thus, one attempts to design an IRS that provides the user with documents that are about the topic(s) as specified in the query.

However, we now know that there are other issues that affect user satisfaction with a document provided by an IRS. There are the factors of the time, cost, and effort to obtain information that affect the user's perception of the IRS. There are a variety of nontopicality factors that the user may take into consideration when doing an evaluation. Here we will mention a few.

A user may be influenced by the author of a document, whether in terms of the author's reputation or whether or not the user has seen enough of that author's work. Also, a user may care about the reputation of the source of the document, i.e., whether or not the source (e.g., a journal or conference proceeding) has a good reputation. A user may worry about the availability of the full text of the document if it is deemed worthy of pursuing, or the readability of the document in question. Other issues of possible concern to a user are the recency of the document or in what language the document is written. A user might be influenced by the citation strength of the article; after all, Google ranks its retrieved web sites in part by the number of inlinks the sites have, as well as other factors such as location, past search history for both the individual searcher and the entire searching community, and the current state of the events at issue. Last, sometimes a user might like an article, even if not all that topical, based on other factors such as the methodology used. In addition, sometimes a user finds an article relevant even when it does not seem to be topical based on serendipity. Clearly, this implies the need to incorporate imprecision into retrieval models (Barry, 1994).

1.4   SOME INTERESTING APPLICATIONS OF INFORMATION RETRIEVAL

The most obvious application is for searching and then retrieving information via documents. Lately, this has been expended to mechanisms for dealing with big data, or extremely large data sets along with issues of data capture, storage, search and retrieval, and analysis (via analytics), as well as data sharing and privacy concern.

Another application area is in the arena of geography. Finding the optimal path from one point to another, via global positioning systems, is one area. One can also determine whether one place is relative to another, i.e., is one address north of another address (this is especially appealing when a city such as New Orleans is laid out in relationship to the meandering Mississippi River).

Of course, the imprecision of such an application begs for the use of fuzzy set theory.

With the increasing use of social media, including blogs, information scientists interested in retrieval have found new avenues of research. One part of this research is related to emotion. For example, in a political blog, do the entries support or argue against a given point of contention.

Related to this is the current concerns over terrorism. Can one identify various terrorist plots, especially when authors of social media messages are clever enough to try to disguise their intentions? Related to this is the retrieval of news stories about various incidents that happen. Clearly, natural language processing has a role as does fuzzy retrieval in these arenas.

Other applications deal with data mining of medical information. Beyond this, the idea of retrieving media beyond text, such as images, videos, and animations, has been a subject of much retrieval research. Sometimes, one considers annotations about images as well as the content of the images. In addition, musical retrieval has found a niche among researchers.

The problems with automatic translation from one language to another shows the issues associated with cross-language retrieval. Can one have a query in one language, e.g., English, and find relevant documents in another language, e.g., Hebrew? For example, the English word "strong" has, according to Google Translate, at least ten different words with nuances of differences. This includes strong in the sense of powerful versus intense or fierce versus spicy or pungent, versus firm or solid, versus courageous, versus violent or aggressive, versus mighty, versus firm or enduring. The imprecision here also could allow for fuzzy retrieval mechanisms.

Also, anyone who has watched television shows about the police has seen retrieval mechanisms used to identify people by DNA or fingerprints or facial recognition. This has led to the use of biometrics, including retina scans, as a means to provide cyber security. The notion of retrieval in such an application area is obvious.

To show that fuzzy set theory has been applied in new and novel ways, consider the fuzzy lookup add-in for Microsoft Office Excel that was developed by Microsoft Research. It performs fuzzy matching of textual data in Excel. It can be used to identify fuzzy duplicate rows within a single table or to fuzzy join similar rows between two different tables. The matching is robust to a wide variety of errors including spelling mistakes, abbreviations, synonyms and added/missing data. For instance, it might detect that the rows containing "Andrew Hill" and the rows containing "Hill, Andrew" or "Andy Hill" all refer to the same underlying entity, returning a similarity score along with each match. While the default configuration works well for a wide variety of textual data, such as product names or customer addresses, the matching may also be customized for specific domains or languages (http://www.excel-university.com/perform-approximate-match-and-fuzzy-lookup-in-excel/).

Modern search engines have included metasearch engines that search a variety of search engines (e.g., http://www.dogpile.com/). This leads to the issue of fusion, eliminating duplicate records. For example, one might find multiple references to the same record, eliminating duplicates by examining the author's name. However, this can prove difficult as the author can be listed in a variety of ways. One of the authors of this book could be listed as "Kraft, D.H.," or "Kraft, Donald H.," or "Kraft, D," and so forth. One way to deal with this is via the Levenshtein distance, the minimum number of single-character edits (i.e., insertions, deletions or substitutions) required to change one word into the other. Another way is to consider fuzzy similarity measures.

One can consider the issue of bibliometrics, including weighting the count of the number of papers by a given author (Zhao and Strotmann, 2016). One could weigh the citations based on a variety of issues, including the frequency of citations. Such weights could be considered fuzzy membership functions for use in evaluating faculty publication records.

Another fascinating application of IR is in the area of software engineering, to be specific, software reuse. Consider an organization having access to a collection of software or related objects (e.g., specifications of requirements, documentation, and testing methodologies). A new request for software comes in, and one can formulate the request as a query to allow for a search of that collection to find elements that can be reused, even if needed to be modified to some extent.

In one study, three extended Boolean models, MMM, Paice, and P-Norm, all of which are discussed in Chapter 2, were employed to model retrieval of software for reuse. While it had previously only been theorized by researchers, it was proven that, in fact, the three extended Boolean models outperformed standard Boolean search. Because the three extended models used term weights to model imprecision, discussed in detail in Chapter 3, we can say those searches were fuzzy. We note that having more query terms present in a given document can lead one to believe that the document in question is more about the concepts represented by those terms, thus increasing the document evaluation, and hence pushing that document higher on the returned list of matches. Fuzzy search is one that takes into consideration the membership function and by looking at the number of times a term appears can be considered one definition of the concept of aboutness (Colvin, 2014).

Searching a UNIX commands database, this research allowed for the recreation of a previous study by Maarek, Berry, and Kaiser in 1991. This study reestablished the data corpus and needed parameters for relevance and non-relevance to be considered (Maarek et al., 1991). The study demonstrated that using the term frequencies improved the overall result of a fuzzy search over a Boolean search (Colvin, 2014).

Other uses have evolved to include the web, as users now want a more personalized experience when they search the web. Personalized Information Retrieval or PIR has evolved in the last decade from the use of keeping contextual information that web browsers now store. This leads to a more personalized resulting list of returned search results when that user on that computer searches the internet compared to another user on another computer searching the exact same query (Ghorab et al., 2013).

Data on the web is interconnected and other ways to search include the Google's Knowledge Graph and other graphs that can search connected data from node to node based on a user's saved information. The biggest difference between the models of IR on the web and traditional IR, is the use of personal information. To return a list personalize to the user, the web search uses the cookies and stored data information that the webpages keep, this along with the queries helps the web search return a better resulting list to the user (Alonso et al., 2015). These new data graphs have led to new data graph search methods in order to connect nodes that might not seem related to the naked eye, but may be the next logical connection due to the users saved preferences, geo-temporal knowledge or social networking information (Alonso et al., 2015).

Users are not only searching the web for information, but also buying and selling items online as well. How do users know if what they are buying is really what is in the picture? They rely on the policy of the website and more and more they are relying on the comments and reviews of other users who have purchased the same item. Manufacturers are taking note of this as well and want to know what people are saying about their product and also their competitor's product. That is how they can improve their products the fastest and fix any bugs that may arise. So how are they finding information that is posted not about their own product but their competitor's product as well? The study, Retrieval of Relevant Opinion Sentences for New Products, in 2015 did a study on searching for terms entered by a user and found a huge success in searching for similar products for products with no reviews and so on. This opens up a whole new field of text mining and term similarity and opportunities that can now be studied on related products and how they are related on the web and how to find them (Park et al., 2015).

1.5   WHERE THE FUZZ IS

The thrust of this book is the application of fuzzy set theory to information retrieval modeling. It seems logical that a reader might ask where the fuzz is. We see fuzz as the idea of imprecision, vagueness, uncertainty, ambiguity, and inconsistency vis-à-vis IR. Very often the terms imprecision, vagueness, uncertainty, and inconsistency are used as synonymous concepts. Nevertheless when they are used to qualify a characteristic of the information they have a distinct meaning.

There are several ways to represent imprecise and vague concepts. One can approach this indirectly by defining similarity or proximity relationships between each pair of imprecise and vague concepts. If we regard a document as an imprecise or vague concept, i.e., as bearing a vague content, a numeric value computed by a similarity measure can be used to express the closeness of any two pairs of documents. This is the way of dealing with the imprecise and vague document and query contents via the weights in IR's vector space model. In this context the documents and the query are represented as points in a vector space of terms and the distances between the query and the documents points are used to quantify their similarity.

Another way to represent vague and imprecise concepts is by means of the notion of fuzzy set. As we shall see, the notion of a fuzzy set is an extension to normal set theory. The notion of fuzzy set has been used in the IR context to represent the vague concepts expressed in a flexible query for specifying soft selection conditions of the documents.

Uncertainty is related to the truth of a proposition, intended as the conformity of the information carried by the proposition with the considered reality. Possibility theory, together with the concept of a linguistic variable defined within fuzzy set theory, provides a unifying formal framework to formalize the management of imprecise, vague and uncertain information.

The same information content can be expressed by choosing a trade-off between the vagueness and the uncertainty embedded in a proposition. A dual representation can eliminate imprecision and augment the uncertainty, like in the expression "it is not completely probable that a given document fully satisfies a given query." One way to model IR is to regard it as an uncertain problem (Kraft et al., 1998).

There are two alternative ways to model IR activity. One possibility is to model the query evaluation mechanism as an uncertain decision process. The concept of relevance is considered binary (crisp), as the query evaluation mechanism computes the probability of relevance of a given document to a given query. Such an approach, which does model the uncertainty of the retrieval process, has been introduced and developed using probabilistic IR models. Another possibility is to interpret the query as the specification of soft "elastic" constraints that the representation of a document can satisfy to an extent, and to consider the term relevant as a gradual (vague) concept. This is the approach adopted in fuzzy IR models. In this latter case, the decision process performed by the query evaluation mechanism computes the degree of satisfaction of the query by the representation of each document. This satisfaction degree, called the retrieval status value (RSV), is considered an estimate of the degree of relevance (or is at least proportional to the relevance) of a given document with respect to a given user query. Traditional IR models consider an RSV of 1 to imply a maximum relevance and an RSV of 0 to imply absolutely no relevance. The introduction of the concept of fuzz allows an RSV in the interval $(0, 1)$, which in turn implies an intermediate level or degree of relevance.

Inconsistency comes from the simultaneous presence of contradictory information about the same reality. An example can be observed when submitting the same query to several IRSs that adopt different representations of documents and produce different results. This is actually very common and often occurs when searching for information over the Internet using different search engines. To solve this kind of inconsistency, some fusion strategies can be applied to the ranked lists each search engine produces. In fact, this is what metasearch engines do.

The document representation based on a selection of index terms is invariably incomplete. When synthesizing the content of a text manually by asking an expert to select a set of index terms, one introduces subjectivity in the representation. On the other hand, automatic full-text indexing introduces imprecision, since the terms are not all fully significant in characterizing a document's content. However, these terms can have a partial significance that might also depend upon the context in which they appear, i.e., which document component. Modern retrieval systems may include natural language processing capabilities to try to deal with semantics. Thus, one can move from the notion of a document as a "bag of terms" to having a set of concepts. This leads to the idea of a taxonomy, i.e., a vocabulary and structure (e.g., a cat is a pet, a dog is a pet), and an ontology, i.e., a set of relationships and rules and constraints (i.e., dogs chase cats). These ideas have their own sets of imprecision or vagueness.

Determining the relationship between data is really subjective. Most studies that use this type of relationship representation of data must rely on users or experts to verify the validity of the data. One recent study used crowdsourcing to gather data when experts weren't available. The best way to get a random group of people to participate in their study was to use crowdsourcing, this was the best way to determine if certain celebrities, who were both actors and directors, were seen as primarily actors or directors by the general public (Bast et al., 2015).

CHAPTER 2

Modeling

An important part of any information retrieval system is the way the system is modeled. In general, modeling is an embodiment of the theory in which we define a set of objects about which assertions can be made and restrict the ways in which classes of objects can interact. A model in information retrieval (IR) specifies the representations used for documents and information needs and how they are queried (Belkin and Croft, 1992). An IR model is a formalization of the way of thinking about information retrieval; one issue in modeling information retrieval is in the area of implementation, determining how to operationalize the model in a given environment (e.g., file structures) (Tamine-Lechani et al., 2010).

Modeling in IR defines the ranking function that will order the documents by match of the search query. Because this is an important and complex process we will first define the relationship between modeling and ranking in IR systems. Each search has a primary target set of data, from a simple web search for general information to specifics like restaurants near a certain location; each can utilize different contextual information to help with the search (Baeza-Yates and Ribeiro-Neto, 2011; Belkin and Croft, 1992). Matching data with a query can be done using different models and sometimes even graphs, because the contextual information can be in any form from text to image to header to title, a search query can search the subject of an email and it's body along with the email addresses to find what it is searching for, all of this is considered contextual information (Minkov et al., 2006).

Every IR system consists of a query, document corpus, and a ranking function of retrieved documents. The necessary part of any information retrieval system is an archive where documents or data are held and a search engine that will retrieve matches of a search query (Kraft et al., 1998).

For each query searched a list of documents retrieved is returned based on how well it matches the query. Matching the documents to the query and predicting which documents the users will find relevant is central problem to all IR systems. The fuzziness comes in how a model defines a match. A Boolean match is considered either exact or not, so if there is no match at all the degree of match is 0, if the word matches exactly in a Boolean system, the match is given a match rank of 1. In fuzzy systems, the degree of match can be varying depending on how the user sets up the weights of terms. For example, a synonym is the same word just written another way, so that may be given the same weighted value as an exact match. If a term is a derivative of a term it may be given a value slightly less than an exact match. These variances or different weights are what make a system fuzzy in a weighted system. Different models rank documents differently using different ranking algorithms in hopes to better solve this problem. All ranking algorithms have similar characteristics although they all include a set of documents (D), set of queries (Q), a ranking function (R(q,d)), and a framework for defining sets, i.e., mapping terms to documents (F). In any IR model "documents" can be records, text, images, video, and so on. Terms can be indicators of concept, dates, authors, publishers, or other items that are being searched.

Consider = D = the set of "documents," i.e., records and T = the set of terms (i.e., keywords). Then, let F = the indexing function mapping terms to documents; F: D X T $\rightarrow$ {0,1}. Consider Q = the set of queries, and let a = the query indexing function mapping terms to q query; a: Q X T $\rightarrow$ {0,1}. One can extend these two mapping functions so that the range becomes [0,1] rather than {0,1}.

Traditional models in IR include Boolean, vector space, probabilistic, and extended Boolean.

2.1   BOOLEAN MODEL

The Boolean model was the first introduced in an online matching system in the early 1960's and 70's. Documents and queries are seen as sets of index terms, of late called "bag of terms." The Boolean search requires an exact match; therefore, queries are usually supplemented with Boolean operators, OR, NOT, or AND. This means query processing consists of set theoretic operations.

The Boolean model in information retrieval is based on the computation Boolean logic. Boolean logic states that everything is either a yes (1) or no (0) with nothing in between. Because this model is simple and intuitive it was widely adopted and was the model used in early systems. With a Boolean OR, a document must contain any of the query terms to satisfy the query. A document must contain all query terms in a Boolean AND query to satisfy the query, or return a 1.

2.1.1   DEFICIENCIES WITH BOOLEAN LOGIC

Using a Boolean model has its advantages in its simplicity of match; a document either contains a term or it doesn't. The issues with the Boolean model are that the matches are not ranked. Therefore, when a match is found, a document may contain a query term one time or one hundred times, there is no ranking system to determine which document has the most occurrences of the term.

For the Boolean OR, there is no preference given to the query terms, the terms all bear the same weight. So there is no way to determine which document contains termA, or termB, or termC. A search may be returned with a match and an equal match may be a different term. Like the algebraic Boolean, there is an order of precedence to the terms, NOT, AND, OR, and they can be changed by the insertion of parenthesis.

Information AND retrieval OR search is not equal to Information AND (retrieval OR search). Matching in a Boolean information retrieval system doesn't allow the relevance of document matches to affect the outcome of the search. If a document contains the searched word once, that document is returned as a match that is equal to a document that contains the word one hundred times. This limitation doesn't always return the most desired results.

One adaptation to this is to add weighted values to documents with more relevant matches. The main limitation to this is in knowing which term to deem a higher value. If searching for a sentence or multiple terms in a phrase, deciding which term gets the highest weighted value is hard to decipher and when a document is returned as a match what is the best way to quantify a qualitative return (Bordogna and Pasi, 1993). Another adaptation is adding weights for specific query terms. For example, if a user searches the Java library for a function that adds two numbers, the keyword in Java is *sum*, but if the user isn't quite sure if it is the keyword or not and is afraid they may miss documents if they only use *sum*, they can put a weight on the word *sum* and search for similar words or expand their query to include *sum* OR *add* OR *plus*. This will give preference to documents that contain *sum*, which is what one would expect being a keyword. This inability to express the importance of terms in a desired document is the main limitation of Boolean search systems (Bordogna et al., 1992).

We can see that in the Boolean logic model, if one searches for two words connected by the Boolean AND, a document with only one word match will be discarded just as a document with no word matches as shown in Table 2.1 (Baeza-Yates and Ribeiro-Neto, 2011; Bookstein, 1980; Fox and Sharan, 1986). In addition, if a query has ten terms ANDed together, a document with nine out of the ten terms is rejected, as is a document with one of the terms. Moreover, if a query has ten terms ORed together, a document with one term is retrieved as is a document with all ten terms.

| Table 2.1: Boolean Truth Table ||||||||
A	B	OR	Value		A	B	AND	Value
T	T	T	1		T	T	T	1
T	F	T	1		T	F	F	0
F	T	T	1		F	T	F	0
F	F	F	0		F	F	F	0

2.2   VECTOR SPACE MODEL

Another common model in IR is the vector space model. Here, the "documents" and the queries are seen as vectors of term weights. Since the term weight are used, instead of a match/no-match system as in the Boolean model, this might be considered related to a fuzzy system. Thus, each dimension is a representation of the possible "document" feature. Introducing the returned matches into a vector-space where documents and queries are represented as vector elements in an n-dimension space. Note that "n" indicates the number of terms. The matching function is the result or the measure of the distance of the result of the query to the document. How far a query lands from the query goal results in a ranked list of outcomes that can then be reevaluated by the user or determined to be a match.

The inability of the Boolean model to rank the results leads to the creation of models that, based on algebraic calculation, can take documents and rank them based on similarity score. The vector space model does this by using index and document term weights and calculating a similarity score for a query. There are many versions of this calculation, but the cosine similarity is usually the best performer of the vector space outcomes and is calculated by

$$sim\,(d_j,\,q_k) = \frac{\sum_{i=1}^{n}(td_{ij}*tq_{ik})}{\sqrt{\sum_{i=1}^{n}td_{ij}*}\sqrt{\sum_{i=1}^{n}td_{ij}*}}\quad,$$

where:

td_{ij} = *the frequency of the ith term in document j*
tq_{ik} = *the frequency of the ith term in the vector for query*
n = *the the number of unique terms in the data set.*

Typically, the weights that are used in the vector space model are the term-frequency, inverse document frequency calculation (TF-IDF) (discussed further in Chapter 3). Because the term weights need to be non-negative and non-binary, the TF-IDF make a good calculation because it is based on the number of times a term is found in a document and the number of times a document is found with the term in the corpus. Creating a term-query pair, the documents (dj) and queries (q) create a t-dimensional vector that represent the data corpus.

$$d_j = (w_{1,j}), w_{2,j},...,w_{1,j}),$$
$$q = (w_{1,q}, w_{2,q},...,w_{1,q})$$

Other calculations include the Jacquard, Dice, and Dot product (Salton et al., 1983).

2.3 PROBABILITY MODEL

The probabilistic model is based on a result and the probability of it meeting the user's needs. It was introduced in 1976 by Robertson and Sparck Jones and many versions have been introduced since (Baeza-Yates and Ribeiro-Neto, 2011). The model says that, based on a resulting set of documents from a query, there is a high probability that one or more answers in the result set will meet the user's needs perfectly or close to perfectly. Since nothing is 100% perfect, how can this be done? How can a system predict what a user wants? The probabilistic model uses only the information that is available to the system, so only the information that the system knows, like the terms in the document. So using the number of times a term is present in a document the system thinks this will make that document more relevant or more interesting to the user. Then ranks the documents based on a relevance calculation. Because the documents are ranked on a relevance calculation or similarity weight, the probabilistic model might be considered related to a fuzzy model. The calculation for the probabilistic model is (Baeza-Yates and Ribeiro-Neto, 2011)

$$\text{sim}(jk) = \Sigma_{i=1}^{Q} (C + \log \frac{N-n_i}{n_i}),$$

where:

Q = the number of matching terms between document j and query k

C = a constant for tuning the probablistic function

n_i = the number of documents having term I in the data set

N = the number of documents in the data set.

However, this, too, has faults. A user may not deem the number of times a term is present to mean that a document is more relevant, or that term may be so common the frequency is basically the same in all documents. In addition, other outside determinants could be present that deem a document to be non-relevant. There are also other terms that can be substituted for terms and have the same meaning or synonyms that are overlooked in a probabilistic model, many other aspects that can affect the outcome of this model returning 100% match.

Based on the results of the probabilistic model, the idea that the user can then select certain responses that do match and return those that don't have lent itself to the creation of models like relevance feedback. Relevance feedback, discussed in detail in Chapter 4, is the idea that using the returned results from a query the user chooses the results that they deem to be relevant and throws back the ones that they do not think are relevant, then those "bad" results get added to the pool of other results and then the query can be run again this time with a better knowledge of what the user is looking for (Frakes and Baeza-Yates, 1992). The user can do this select/throwback until they are satisfied that they are getting all the results or that they are receiving the most relevant results the system has to offer.

The three models discussed so far have been under the premise that the indexed terms are independent of each other. Independence among index terms can be restrictive, instead if the index terms are composed of smaller pieces, all derived from one corpus, and has led to the interpretation of the generalized vector space model. The generalized vector space model says that in a collection of terms or given vocabulary, there is a min-term (or conjunctive component) and then we can associate a vector with each min-term (Baeza-Yates and Ribeiro-Neto, 2011). This idea leads to idea of nets and more specifically neural nets and Bayesian inference nets.

2.3.1 LANGUAGE MODELS

Language models are widely used in IR systems with the probabilistic method to help determine the next part of speech. Usually language models work better than traditional vector models because typical speech patterns or speech terms are found together and so prediction of the next term is easier than a search term in a corpus of random data. Basically, this means determining the likelihood of a given string occurring in a given language. This could modify the probabilities of a document being relevant to a query having the given string. Issues include whether terms in the string are treated as statistically independent as opposed to the use of conditional probabilities.

Clearly, there is an opportunity to add fuzziness in terms of possibility functions as opposed to probabilities. This can be used, as seen in Chapter 5, to expand the query with semantically related terms.

2.3.2 ALTERNATIVE PROBABILISTIC BEST MATCH MODELS

There are other plays on the probabilistic model include the BM1, BM11, BM15, and BM25 models. These models are similar and stand for Best Match, the most common is the BM25. The BM25 model works great with plain text documents and has been proven itself at TREC. The BM25 model looks at how often a term is in a document and the average document length in the corpus (Robertson et al., 2004). The BM25 also has two boosting variables that are commonly set at k = 2 and b = .75 for best results. All variations of the BM models use the term-frequency factor and a document length normalizer. This takes into consideration the length of the document as a measure of how many times the term is in the document, so if the term is in the document 25 times but the document has 100 words, that would rank the same as a document that had the term appear 1 time in a document with 4 words (Robertson et al., 2004).

Entering queries can be a tricky task that can change the outcome of a search. Query expansion is the manipulation of similar words or placement of words in the query to search for the same idea just using different terminology that may match the corpus better. Query expansion is usually discussed along with relevance feedback as feedback methods. An example of a query expansion looks like this: sum OR add OR plus, words with the same meaning are ORed together to return any document that may include them (Xu and Croft, 1996).

2.4   MODERN CONCEPTS OF IR

Croft et al. (2010) use the phrase "beyond bag of words" to refer to the notion that retrieval can go beyond a simple representation of text as a collection or bag of words. This includes issues of linguistics (i.e., natural language), metadata, and media content. It allows for techniques such as SVM (support vector machine), which is a method for classification based on hyperplanes and supervised learning.

One aspect is the notion of using features to score documents as related to queries for the purpose of ranking. Some of these features could be term occurrences and term frequencies, term proximities, and document lengths. Another aspect is the incorporation of term dependencies. It is known that terms are related (see Chapter 5 for a discussion of the use of fuzzy rough sets to model such dependencies).

There has been some work on retrieval of objects representing given entities. For example, given the query about cancer treatments, one could retrieval articles on chemotherapy chemicals or centers where such are administered to patients. In addition, some work has been done on searching literature to find relationships between illnesses and treatments.

A recent innovation is the use of XML (Extensible Markup Language, which can be used to encode documents so that they are both human and machine readable). There has been a body of research on retrieval based on XML representations of documents. Research has looked at using many aspects of the XML language, the XPath by Marrara et al. (2011) and FleX-Path by Damiani et al. (2008). Each looked at how the XML allows users to search for content based keywords or specific constraints on the document, because XML can be fragmented to support both formats. This ability to search a document on the document format or content it holds opens new possibilities and an extra layer for information retrieval not before seen, documents can now be searched on either/or rather than on one specified format and allows flexible constraints to be entered. The resulting list of ranked XML fragments appears in the same format as the query. Using XML is not uncommon as it is a common web-based extension and allows real-time alterations to occur and also allows one to formulate search criteria that is structured and also flexible enough to change dynamically while still produce promising results.

The idea of having so much data on the web about so many topics and being able to be quickly changed when needed is referred to as soft computing, more specifically soft computing is defined by procedures and practices that work together to retrieve information effectively that is relevant and applicable to the user's needs (Herrera-Viedma and Pasi, 2006). Web pages and cloud data banks store an enormous amounts of information about users, services, and items, and also about user behavior in reaction to certain web actions like maintenance, sales, font change, etc. This idea of how to provide fast, reliable responses is on every websites agenda when designing any type of web presence. Getting the data, the user wants to the user the fastest and predicting with the most certainty what the user will want first is the ultimate goal of all web sites. Because soft computing represents an ideal platform for information retrieval and an effective IRS, there is much research into the creation of IRSs for the web and they usually include tools using fuzzy set theory.

Adding to complexity of web-searching, there are many other studies that look at other factors that deal with how users search the web. DaCosta Pereira et al. (2009) look at a web search as an individual information retrieval application and instead of sticking to only the terms in the query, allow the user to have some "aboutness" in their search terms. This means that searches that include multiple criteria may ultimately result in no results and 100% non-compliance results, so they said what if the compliance was ok not matching 100%. If a user searches for books by Dr. Seuss written before 1970, they may be happy with only getting results of books written by Dr. Seuss. Because of the way the data can be stored on the web, either locally or remotely, the web presents a whole new way to look at data and Information Retrieval Systems. Bordogna et al. (2003) also looked at this and presented both factions, the web as a unique, large data corpus and then again each search as individual IRSs. Then fused the resulting lists together to see if this proposed a better solution at finding a match. From this though, two issues arise as one would imagine, document retrieval size, i.e. how many documents do you allow to be retrieved? And second, from which do you prioritize the matches to populate the resulting list.

Searching multiple search engines and getting multiple ranked lists of returned results is a problem not new to researchers. Optimizing the combination of the documents is something that is looked at analyzed using the fuzzy set theory that adapts a quantifier guided Ordered Weighed Averaging (OWA) operators. These operators, originally introduced by Yager, are used to evaluate alternative measurements for missing or partially missing documents (missing in some searches but not all) in order to place all documents in an ordered list before ranking them all together. A study by Diaz et al. (2005) showed much improved results over the standard strategy when this method was applied.

In addition, work has been done on automatic summarization and recommender systems. Moreover, especially in the area of artificial intelligence, work has been done on question/answer systems.

In recent years the term crowdsourcing has become popular and popular with data scientists. Crowdsourcing is using the information of a large group as the source of information or as the data corpus for a study or advertising or the such. Using a model based on the probabilistic model called the Bradley-Terry model which uses the law of transitivity to say that if user A likes X and X is equal to Y then user A likes Y (Bradley and Terry, 1952). This method of crowdsourcing has become popular in information retrieval and using the probabilistic model, researchers can now predict to some certainty what a user may want for new spring colors, or new car designs based on old patterns. Chen et al. (2013) use this model to infer a new way to rank selections or documents from a corpus of data. Using the data from a crowdsourced group, they were able to deduce a much faster way to asses a predictors outcome. This allows predictor systems recommend the next step or next piece of data quicker and more accurately because if a group of people can react to a webpage ad stating they like product Y, and all users from town C like product Y and product Z is very similar to product Y then it's safe to say it should be marketed in town C in order to ensure good sales. Using this method for recommender systems will benefit different types of services like marketing companies and even military operations (Chen et al., 2013).

In all of these modern approaches, there are the notions of uncertainty, ambiguity, and imprecision, leading to the possibility of modeling using fuzzy set theory.

2.5   FUZZY LOGIC AND SETS

In a traditional set, the transition from one set to another is clear, distinct, or crisp. The membership of an item in a set is clearly defined. In some cases, that membership is not so clear, having rather indistinct or blurred lines. Membership can belong to multiple groups or sets; this is considered a fuzzy set. If the membership has a varying degree of belonging, is described with vagueness and ambiguity, it is a fuzzy set. Fuzzy sets lead to fuzzy logic, and in fuzzy logic there are three common operators, union, complement, and intersection.

Zadeh is credited with the integration of fuzzy logic into the world of computation and IR. Because of fuzzy logic, we are able to calculate these things instead of writing them off as being luck of the draw, or by chance. For example, if you wanted to find someone who was "very tall" and 95% of the boys on the basketball team are over 7′ tall, if you were to pick a boy from the basketball team you would have a very high chance to pick a very tall person. But if 95% of the cheerleaders were under 5′6″, there would be a very low chance you would pick a very tall person if you were to pick from that pool. But, what is tall? How big must one's height be to be considered tall?

2.6   MEMBERSHIP FUNCTIONS

Just as there are more than one way to represent the data, there is more than one way to represent the membership function that corresponds to that data. Using mathematics or just one's intuition, the membership function assignments can be based on intuition, inference, rank ordering, neural networks, genetic algorithms, or inductive reasoning.

2.6.1   INTUITION

Intuition is no more than using one's own contextual and semantic knowledge about a topic and putting them all together to create membership functions that make sense. For example, if the measurements are feet and inches for height or hot, cold, or rainy, might belong to a function called weather.

2.6.2   INFERENCE

Inference includes using what we know about a topic to infer what we don't know. For example, we know the three inside angles add to be 180° in a triangle, if any of the angles = 90° it's a right triangle, if all angles = 60° it's an equilateral, etc.

2.6.3 RANK ORDERING

Rank ordering requires the outcome of a procedure or a voting by a user or group or committee to determine which order to put the outcomes in. Then based on the number of votes and number of options, it can be decided which variable will go into which function. For example, if you queried the elementary school for their favorite color candies, red, green, yellow, green, you should get a list in order of which color had the most votes to the least votes.

2.6.4 NEURAL NETWORKS

The neural network model works like a neural network to continuously modify itself until either an ideal situation is created or no more situations can be created. Using multiple sets of data points, the network will continue to check and train itself. Then the membership function is determined by mapping the result grouping the overlapping results together.

2.6.5 GENETIC ALGORITHMS

Like neural networks, the genetic algorithm used for a membership function is a survival of the fittest. The algorithm will continuously check itself until a desired result is found or there are no more options left to check. The membership function will end up being the last value or the best fitness value. This concept is discussed in detail for IR in Chapter 4.

2.6.6 INDUCTIVE REASONING

Using a base line drawn between two classes of sample data, inductive reasoning uses the assumption that the database does not change and that the answer will be found within those lines. The lines become the threshold value and as those lines are evaluated and redrawn closer and closer eventually a best fit answer is found.

2.6.7 AGGREGATION

Aggregation means the combining of views, for example using AND OR to get a better result. It is seen that it is better to evaluate a document on each term separately and then aggregate them according to the Boolean structure of the query, preserving the homogeneity of the model.

Consider some functions F:D x T→[0,1] mapping terms to documents and a:Q x T mapping terms to queries. One can treat F and a as importance weights so g:F x a → [0,1] as an RSV for just one specific term, and g = f*a. This does not work for a query with two terms combined with an AND if one term has a large value of a and the other has a small value of a. Another possibility is considering a threshold rule where g = P(a)*F/a if F<a and g = P(a)+Q(a)*(F-a)/(1-a) otherwise. _Or, one can consider the weights as an ideal so g = $e^{K*(F-a)*(F-a)}$. Finally, one can combine these functions, so g= P(a)* $e^{K*(F-a)*(F-a)}$ if F<a and g == P(a)+Q(a)*(F-a)/(1-a) otherwise. Note that P(a) and Q(a) are parameters given as functions of the value of a, and K is a parameter less parameter.

For aggregation functions there is a whole theory involving t-norms for AND and t-co-norms for OR. Common for an AND is the minimum function, for an OR is the maximum function, and for a NOT is a 1- function. Aggregation may or may not increase the result a user is looking for, so the option to weight one or more of the terms has been studied, called Ordered Weighted Average (OWA) (Yager, 1988). Bordogna and Pasi (1993) generated the semantics of OWA for various parameters.

Another model is proposed for aggregating multiple criteria for relevance on documents. This model uses a proportional look using the satisfaction degree of criterion to prioritize the criteria on the multidimensional property of documents. The criteria are measured on how well they satisfy they match the following relevance: aboutness, coverage, appropriateness and reliability (Pereira et al., 2012). Using the satisfaction degree, this model allows the system to use the higher priority criteria more heavily weighted than those criteria that are less priority or less satisfying.

2.7   EXTENDED BOOLEAN IN IR

The Boolean vector space and probabilistic models are not the only options when it comes to an IR system. There are three additional models that are considered extended Boolean because they combine the term weights and membership functions of a fuzzy set model and return matches that as accurate as a Boolean model. The models, all involved with extending the Boolean model in information retrieval, are the MMM (Min, Max, and Mixed), the Paice model, and the P-Norm.

The MMM model is loosely based on the fuzzy set notion that was originally proposed by Zadeh. The MMM model was developed by Fox and Sharat in 1986 and says each term has a fuzzy set that it is associated with it (Frakes and Baeza-Yates, 1992). The MMM model says that an element, i.e., each indexed term, has a varying membership to a data set but only looks at the min and max document weights for the index term (Frakes and Baeza-Yates, 1992). Moreover, the weight of a document with respect to an index term is considered to be the degree of membership of the document in the fuzzy set associated with it.

Using the term frequency calculation (tf/idf) as the term weight, the MMM is calculated by:

SIM (or Q_{or},D) = $C_{or\,1}$ * max (tf/idf of queried terms) + $C_{or\,2}$ * min (tf/idf of queried terms)

SIM (or Q_{and},D) = $C_{and\,1}$ * min (tf/idf of queried terms) + $C_{and\,2}$ * max (tf/idf of terms) .

Here, Q is the query with an OR or with an AND, D is the document with index-term weights tf/idf, and C is a coefficient for "softness," this model gives the most importance during the AND queries to the maximum of the documents and the minimum the highest of important during the OR queries. Usually, $C_{and\,2}$ is just 1 - $C_{and\,1}$ and $C_{or\,2}$ is calculated as 1 - $C_{or\,1}$.

The Paice model was proposed by Paice in 1984, and is also based on the fuzzy set theory (Frakes and Baeza-Yates, 1992). Similar to the MMM model, the Paice model looks at the weighted indexes in the document but doesn't stop at the min and the max like the MMM model, it considers all of the weights of the document. The Paice similarity is calculated by

SIM (Q, D) = $\sum_{i=1}^{n} r^{i-1}\,d_i / \sum_{i=1}^{n} r^{i-1}$,

where n = number of queries, Q is the query and d is the tf/idf for the document for an OR query, D = (A_1 or A_2 or ... or A_n) where A is the tf/idf for query term 1, etc. and for an AND query, D = (A_1 and A_2 or ... and A_n).

The p-norm model adds another angle to the Paice model by considering the weight of the query as well as the weights of the documents (Frakes and Baeza-Yates, 1992). In the research it has been found that p = 2 gives good results, for this research, the weight used will be 2. The p-norm model for an ORed query is

SIM($Q_{or\,p}$, D = $((a_1^p d_{A1}^p + a_2^p d_{A2}^p + ... + a_n^p d_{An}^p)/(a_1^p + a_2^p + ... + a_n^p))$,

where Q is the query, D is the document, a is the term weight d is the document weight, p is set to 2, and A is the term for which the document weight is corresponding. For an ANDed query the model is:

SIM ($Q_{and\,p}$,D) = $\sqrt[p]{((a_1^p(1 - d_{A1}) + a_2^p(1 - d_{A2})^p + ... + a_n^p(1 - d_{An}))/(a_1^p + a_2^p + ... + a_n^p))}$.

2.8 FUZZY EVALUATION METRICS

2.8.1 MAP

To determine if a similarity measure is doing a better job than another there needs to be a measure to compare. The most common measure in an IR system is using the recall and precision. Recall is defined as the proportion of relevant documents that are retrieved and precision is the proportion of a retrieved set of documents that are actually relevant. These measures are inversely related, as precision goes up, recall goes down and vice versa. Recall = $|A \cap B|/|A|$ and precision = $|A \cap B|/|B|$, where A is the number of relevant document and B is the number of retrieved documents. The degree of precision is not a number that is easily calculated, one way precision can be calculated is to look at specific cutoff points in the returned ranked list.

The more precise the match is, i.e., the more specific the query gets, often it is the case that the less recall will be, and vice versa. For example, if a search is for *sum function* there should be plenty of matches returned, so low precision and high recall. If the term *integer* gets added to the query *sum function*, the more precise the returned solutions will be, but the number of items returned will be less.

Of course, one can generate fuzzy precision and recall. Fuzzy recall = $\Sigma_{i \in D}$ $min(e_i,r_i)/\Sigma_{i \in D}r_i$ and Fuzzy precision = $\Sigma_{i \in D}min(e_i,r_i)/\Sigma_{i \in D}e_i$, where e_i = the RSV for document i and r_i = the user's evaluation of the relevance of document i, and D = the set of documents.

The mean average precision (or MAP) is a widely used measure that results in a single numerical figure that represents the effectiveness of a system (Turpin and Scholer, 2006). The MAP is just the average of all the individual precisions divided by the total number of queries. With a single measure of quality across recall values, multiple systems can now be compared to each. MAP is defined as

$$\text{Average Precision} = \frac{\Sigma_{r=1}^{N}(P(r) X \, rel(r))}{\# \, Relevant \, documents}$$

$$\text{Mean Average Precision} = \frac{AP}{Q},$$

where Q is the total number of queries, N is the number of retrieved documents, r is the rank in the sequence of retrieved documents, $P(r)$ is the precision at rank r, and $rel(r)$ is 1 if the item at r is relevant and 0 if it is not. MAP is a stable way to compare different measures across multiple IR systems that use different search algorithms.

It is noteworthy that recall can be compared to (1-α) where α = Type I error in statistical decision theory, and precision can be compared to (1-β) where β – Type II error. The Neyman-Pearson lemma says one is to maximize precision subject to a constraint that recall $\geq \alpha$. We also note that recall is difficult to measure, and that precision can be related to search length.

Two other statistics are G = Generality is the proportion of documents that are relevant, and Fa = fallout = the proportion of non-relevant documents that are retrieved. We note that the notion that an act of retrieval should convey relevance information, i.e., precision $\geq$ generality, is a weak condition. In addition, once can combine measures so that E = 1 - 1/[a/precision + (1-a)/recall] and F= (1+a)*precision*recall/ (a*precision+recall), where a is a user specified parameter. Note that a>1 emphasizes precision while a<1 emphasizes recall.

2.9 DISCOUNTED CUMULATIVE GAIN

Another commonly used measure for web searches is discounted cumulative gain, (DCG). Discounted cumulative gain relies on two assumptions: (1) that documents are ranked by relevance in a search and (2) that documents ranked higher in the list are more relevant than the documents listed below it (Dupret, 2011). Discounted cumulative gain is written as

$$DCG_P = rel_i + \sum_{i=2}^{p} \frac{rel_i}{log_2 (i)} ,$$

where rel_i is the graded relevance of the result at position i. For example if the user provides relevance scores of 3, 2, 3, 0, 1, and 2. Which means document 1 has a relevance score of 3, document 2 has a relevance score of 2, and so on. The sum of the relevance scores divided by the log (base 2) will be

$$DCG6 = reli + \sum_{i=2}^{p} \frac{rel_i}{log_2 (i)} = 3 + (2 + 1.89 + 0 + 0.43 + 0.77) = 8.10.$$

Another measures used in conjunction with the results of the DCG for web-based searches include Deterministic Click Model and Probabilistic Click Models. Each of these count the number of or predict the number of times a user clicks a specific page, given the results of a specific search engines results. These are used to validate that the DCG or MAP are correct in that the results given by a search are in fact, what a user actually searched.

2.10 SUMMARY

There are many models that can be used for an IR system and they all provide a different way to represent the data. The Boolean model uses the traditional AND, OR, and NOT to query a corpus for term being present (1) or not (0). This model is effective but can be very size costly and return a large amount of matched documents. The vector space model is a more fuzzy approach than as it considers the distance between two terms in a vector space as a weight to determine the similarity. It also turns the corpus into an n-dimensional vector and plots the result of the query, the closer to the result the better. The probabilistic model, considered to also be fuzzy because it as well uses a weighted measure of similarity, says that there is a probability that is can find a match to the user's needs based on its similarity calculation. And the extended Boolean models all take a different weighting approach to calculate the weight for the term frequency in a document to calculate the similarity measure.

Fuzzy sets in IR adds an alternative to the traditional inclusion of the Boolean logic. Now instead of a term belonging or not to one data set, it can have a degree of membership to one or more data set.

If the membership has a varying degree of belonging, is described with vagueness and ambiguity, it is a fuzzy set. Using the MAP, and the recall and precision measure, multiple IR search algorithms can be compared to each other. There are other measures for IR systems including discounted cumulative gain, deterministic click models, and probabilistic click models.

CHAPTER 3

Source of Weights

The traditional information retrieval (IR) system consists of set of documents or data corpus that is to be searched for the user's query. This set of documents can be anything from text documents to book titles with author, to images, song pages, entire books, and these sets can be quite large. Imagine the entire local library and try to find one or two desired documents there. Most of the recent IR systems consist of documents that are indexed with a vocabulary of keywords. Keywords are usually a word or phrase that can quickly and uniquely identify an element in the set with ease. For example, keywords can be part of a book title, book author, ISBN number, song title, or the date a piece of art was created. Indexes consisting of the keywords with links to the documents in which they occur can make searching easier.

The idea of adding weights came from Luhn but has been researched by many (Baeza-Yates and Ribeiro-Neto, 2011). The basic premise is that any term in a document will be given a weight based on how many times that term is in the document, of course the more times a term appears in the document the higher the term weight would be. It is assumed that documents with a high weight for a specific term would be the most desirable in a search for that term (Baeza-Yates and Ribeiro-Neto, 2011). Other forms of term weights includes putting weights on query terms, so specific search terms have more meaning than others, and a combination of the two where weights are put on both the terms in the index and on the query terms.

3.1   INDEXING

A typical index is a list of keywords or a stemmed version of the keyword. Stemming is combining words with a common root but different suffixes together. For example, the terms "stopping" and "stopped" would be stemmed to the root "stop." This allows one to add occurrences of such terms together for the root term in an index. The index would consist of the term and the number of times each word is found in the corpus, as well as a link to the documents in which the term occurs. This allows a faster look up for a quicker search.

These indexes cannot only provide a faster way to search but also provide a source of weights for any query that the user may want to create but have one word with more important than another. For example, if the query is *information AND re-*

trieval but the word user feels that the term *search* could also be included. If the user weights the terms information and *retrieval* with a higher weight and the term *search* with a lower weight, even though *search* is found in a document the same number of times a document contains the term *information*, the document containing the term *information* would be returned higher in the list of returned documents because of the weights assigned.

Returned list of documents in the order that they are ranked:

Doc 1	Doc 2
Information is the heart of the web	*Search* the web to find a web of data

There are other ways to index a document and these other versions of indexing come into play when the documents are of a differing size, content, and structure. On the web, multimedia documents for example can be big, small, a picture, a movie, etc. Bordogna and Pasi (2001) looked at having the user define the indexing in a hierarchical indexing system for web-based multimedia documents. When dealing with special files, hierarchical might be the only common factor that helps tie them together to get a good index for searching. This was able to be applied to other specialty documents—any semi-structure document they found was able to fit this personalized model. This personalized model has to be done at the indexing level and allows personalized views to shape the indexing of the document based on how the user sees the content or the document structure (Bordogna and Pasi, 2005).

One interesting aspect of differing indexing approaches that was discovered is that the more generic a document is represented by its content, the less effective any indexing will be. This is pretty intuitive to think that if one represents a document with only the vaguest of terms, the less likely it will match a very specific query, but the comparison to a structured document representation proved to be widely more responsive even when a fuzzy representation was given (Bordogna and Pasi, 1995).

3.1.1   TF-IDF

The most popular term weighting scheme is TF-IDF. The term frequency is calculated as simply $tf_{i,j} = f_{i,j}$, where t = term and f = frequency of a term i in document j. There are many variants that have been created on this, the most common using the logarithm to the base 2, so then $tf_{i,j} = 1 + \log f_{i,j}$, if $f_{i,j} > 0$. An example of this calculation is in Table 3.1 using the two documents above.

Table 3.1: Term frequencies				
Term	$f_{i,1}$	$f_{i,2}$	$tf_{i,1}$	$tf_{i,2}$
the	2	1	2	1
web	1	2	1	2
of	1	1	1	1
data	0	1	-	1
information	1	0	1	-
is	1	0	1	-
heart	0	1	-	1
to	0	1	-	1
find	0	1	-	1
search	0	1	-	1
Document Size	7	10		

The phrase IDF stands for inverse document frequency, which is how many times the term was found in the document as compared to its occurrences in the collection. The IDF is calculated by taking log of the total number of documents in the corpus or collection divided by the number of documents that have the specific term that you are searching. For example if we are looking for the TF-IDF for the word web in the example above,

IDF = $\log_2$ (number of documents in the corpus/number of documents that contain search term). For example, the IDF for the term "web" in document 1 = $\log_2$ (2/1) = $\log_2$ (2) = 1. The TF*IDF of "web" for document 2 = 2 * 1 = 2.

3.2   VARIANTS

There are many variants to the standard TF-IDF calculation, which can be used and have been used in the literature. Salton, Buckley, Witten, Moffat, and Bell, just to name a few, have used other versions and some of those variant versions include binary, raw frequency, log normalization (which we just discussed), double normalization .5, and double normalization K (Frakes and Baeza-Yates, 1992). The variants are described in Table 3.2.

Table 3.2: TF weighting calculations

TF Variant	Weighting Calculation
Binary	0, 1
Raw frequency	Just frequency, $f_{i,j}$
Log normalization	As shown above, $1 + \log f_{i,j}$
Double normalization 0.5	$0.5 + 0.5 \dfrac{f_{i,j}}{\max_{i,f_{i,j}}}$
Double normalization K	$K + (1 - K) \dfrac{f_{i,j}}{max_{i,f_{i,j}}}$

Variants to the IDF calculation are similar and include unary, inverse frequency, inverse frequency smooth, inverse frequency max, and probabilistic inverse frequency.

Table 3.3: IDF weighting calculations

IDF Variant	Weighting Calculation
unary	1
Inverse frequency	$\log \dfrac{N}{n_i}$
Inverse frequency smooth	$\log(1 + \dfrac{N}{n_i})$
Inverse frequency max	$\log(1 + \dfrac{max_{in_i}}{n_i})$
Probabilistic Inverse frequency	$\log \dfrac{N - n_i}{n_i}$

Here, N = the number of documents and n_i = the number of documents with term t_i occurring at least once.

The TF calculation should be matched to the IDF scheme used to get a standard calculation. However, there can be many different variations to the calculations of TF-IDF. Salton proposed the following TF-IDF calculations use d together in order to maintain a suitable calculation across document collections (Salton et al., 1983).

Table 3.4: TF-IDF calculations

Scheme	Document weight scheme
1	$f_{i,j} * \log \dfrac{N}{n_i}$
2	$1 + \log f_{i,j}$
3	$(1 + \log f_{i,j}) * \log \dfrac{N}{n_i}$

3.2.1   DOCUMENT LENGTH NORMALIZATION

Another part of a document collection that could be considered when looking at weighting and ranking terms is the length of a document. Document length can also be normalized, and to do this we divide the rank of the document by the length of the document. Documents can be normalized not just by number of terms, but also by bytes, size, etc. It's dependent on the type of document and data that is being stored.

For example if a term is present in a document 100 times and that document contains 32,000 words, in a search result that document might be at the top of the list since the term is found 100 times. Especially if the next closest document contains the term 13 times, but has a length of 2,000. If we divide the number of times a term is found by the length of the document the first document has a term frequency of .003 and the second document has a term frequency of .0065. So based on the ratio of words to term instances, the second document is actually a better match.

One other alternative is to ignore frequency and base the index weights on the subjective opinion of the indexer.

3.3   QUERYING

Creating a query that is meaningful and informative and that will return the best result is not the easiest task. The most common search is for a single term, usually the term is located in the index and a returned list of the documents where that term is found is returned in a ranked order from highest to lowest based on how often the term appears. If the index is not big enough to hold all the data, or only contains the document numbers of those documents containing the searched term, a follow-up search will then be performed to search that list of documents to count the number of occurrences of the term in each document.

Two term queries it is considered conjunctive (uses the Boolean AND operator) or disjunctive (uses the Boolean OR operator). Conjunctive queries are common for searching the web and other large data collections as it is a great way to eliminate most of the returned data. Chapter 2 goes into Boolean logic and how the AND and OR work. In order to best utilize the conjunctive and disjunctive features of a search, it's best to use the disjunctive search for including synonyms that could possibly be used for a specific term, for example, *data OR Information AND retrieval OR search*. And it's best to use the conjunctive search for terms that are not similar but are needed and you are looking for together in the same document.

With the query *Information AND retrieval*, one is searching for documents that contain both terms, documents that contain just one of these terms may not even relate to the subject of information retrieval and therefore may be irrelevant. So, to make sure both terms are in retrieved documents together, one uses a conjunctive query.

There is the possibility to put as many words together as you like in a query, and like any mathematical equation, the use of parenthesis changes the order of precedence. There are many ways to construct a query and many algorithms and tools out there to help construct the best query to get the best results. Because the data is subjective, what is relevant to one user may not be relevant to another user so deciding which method is not an easy problem to solve. Trial and error is also the best option if there are multiple word phrases, although contextual phrases are a little easier to search than regular two word searches, because it's easy to map certain words together, i.e., snow storm vs. snow temperature.

Salton's proposal for the TF-IDF calculations could have query weights used together with the index weights, as seen in Table 3.5.

Table 3.5: Document weighting schemes	
Scheme	**Document weight scheme**
1	$(0.5 + 0.5 \frac{f_{i,j}}{max_{if_{ij}}}) * \log \frac{N}{n_i}$
2	$\log(1 + \frac{N}{n_i})$
3	$(1 + \log f_{i,j}) * \log \frac{N}{n_i}$

It may be the case that the user might be asked for a subjective estimate for query weights, since frequency of terms in the query are usually either 0 or 1. Users often simply do not bother with such subjective weights, simply using an implied 0 if the term in question is not in the query, and 1 if the term is in the query.

Query weights can come in many different forms, implicit, relative importance, threshold, and ideal to name a few.

Implicit query weights uses the Boolean query language and the returned ranked list of documents based on a user's query in descending order. Using the soft constraint associated with the pair <t, 1> the term closest to 1, with the evaluation $\mu_w(F(d,t)) = F(d,t)$ will be the document that is the best match (Tamir et al., 2015), i.e., where t is a single term, and d is a document.

Relative importance query weights looks at terms with relative importance as they relate to other terms in the query. This allows documents with higher index term weights to be ranked higher in the returned list of results. Because terms are compared to each other the concept of separability is lost using this method. Based on the Boolean operator used, there are two definitions for these queries: for disjunctive queries the first proposal is $\mu_w(F(d,t)) = [w * F(d, t)]$ for disjunctive queries and $\mu_w(F(d,t)) = \max(1, F(d, t)/w)$ for conjunctive queries, while the second proposal is $\mu_w(F(d,t)) = \min[w, F(d, t)]$ for disjunctive queries and $\mu_w(F(d,t)) = \max[(1 - w), F(d, t)]$ for conjunctive queries (Tamir et al., 2015). By using these definitions, any weighted Boolean query can be expressed in disjunctive normal form (DNF) (Tamir et al., 2015).

Threshold query weights allow the issue of separability to remain a non-issue by saying, give me all the documents that relate to this topic. Then the threshold can be increased or decreased or "tightened" to increase how over and under the results will be, of course the lower the threshold the more documents will be returned and vice versa. Using a crisp threshold, the basic equation for the threshold query point is for w, where d is a document, t is a term, and w is the minimum weight value set that documents must contain.

$$\mu_w(F(d,t)) = \begin{cases} 0, & \text{for} \quad F(d,t) < w \\ F(d,t) & \text{for} \quad F(d,t) \geq w \end{cases},$$

Because this does not always yield a consistent number of successfully relevant document and the number of documents can change with the slightest change in weights, it has been proposed to use the following instead

$$\mu_w(F(d,t)) = \begin{cases} P(w) * \dfrac{F(d,t)}{w} & \text{for} \quad F(d,t) < w \\ P(w) + Q(w) * \dfrac{F(d,t) - w}{(1 - w)} & \text{for} \quad F(d,t) \geq w \end{cases},$$

where $P(w)$ and $Q(w)$ might be defined as $P(w) = \frac{1+w}{2}$ and $Q(w) = \frac{1-w^2}{4}$. For $F(d,t) < w$, the μ_w function measures the closeness of $F(d,t)$ to w; for $F(d,t) \geq \mu_w (F(d,t))$ expresses the degree of over satisfaction with respect to w, and under satisfaction with respect to 1 (Tamir et al., 2015).

Ideal query weights measures how close each document come close to a perfect document based on a pair <t, w> with the calculation for the soft constraint μ_w, as

$$\mu_w(F(d,t)) = e^{\,1n(k)*(F(d,t)-w)^2}$$

Here, the Gaussian functions slopes are used to measure the steepness of the parameter K in the pair [0, 1] (Tamir et al., 2015). As k decreases the soft constraint becomes stronger and "closer to w" (Tamir et al., 2015). "The retrieval operation associated with a pair <t,w> corresponds in this model to the evaluation of a similarity measure between the importance value w and the significance value of t in R_d: w $\approx$ F(d,t)" (Tamir et al., 2015, p. 282).

3.4   SUMMARY

The source of weights in any IR system can come from multiple places. The most common is the frequency of the term in the document. This is used with the number of documents in a corpus. The number of documents a term is present is the TF-IDF and it is a popular IR weighing scheme. Weighing could be done on the term, or even on the document itself, which allows for a preference for terms or documents in a search. It can also help the ranking of returned search results as a result of a query. There are many variant of the TF-IDF, the most common is the log formalization inverse frequency.

Queries need to be created using a vocabulary that is related to the data corpus. There are multiple ways to create queries. Single-word queries may not return the best result so multiple words can be queried together connected by the Boolean operators AND, OR, and NOT to include or eliminate documents that contain all words, only one word, or one but not the other word.

CHAPTER 4

Relevance Feedback and Query Expansion

4.1 DEFINING RELEVANCE FEEDBACK

Suppose that a user has approached an IRS with a specific query for information, and the system has responded with a list of documents, or at least their representations, perhaps in ranked order. The user looks over the list and determines which of the retrieved items are relevant to his/her query. However, the user wants more relevant items. Relevance feedback allows the IRS to modify the search and redo the matching of documents to the query.

It is usually the case that it is the query that is modified in such a way as to retrieve more items that are like those that the user deemed as relevant while avoiding retrieval of items that are like those that the user deemed as nonrelevant. While there has been a bit of research into modifying the document representations, i.e., indexing weights, we will concentrate in this book on query modification.

4.2 PSEUDO-RELEVANT FEEDBACK

It is noteworthy that there has been work on what is known as pseudo-relevant feedback. This is where the IRS's ranking is used to infer relevance, i.e., the higher the ranking, the more relevant the item is. While not perfect, it does allow the IRS to avoid bothering the user with having to make a lot of relevance judgments.

4.3 RELEVANCE FEEDBACK WITH THE VECTOR SPACE MODEL

Recall that with the vector space model, the query and all documents are represented as points in the vector space of the terms in the vocabulary. The concept of relevance feedback consists of moving the query closer to the documents deemed relevant by the user while moving the query away from the documents deemed nonrelevant by the user.

Mathematically, the model yields

$$q' = q + \alpha \Sigma_{i \in R} d_i + (1 - \alpha) \Sigma_{i \in R'} d_i \, ,$$

where q is the original query representation in the vector space, q' is the modified query representation in the vector space, R is the set of documents deemed relevant, and R' is the set of documents deemed nonrelevant. Moreover, α is a parameter in the range [0,1] that allows the IRS to vary the importance of the relevant document set versus the importance of the nonrelevant document set when it comes to moving the query.

4.4 RELEVANCE FEEDBACK WITH THE PROBABILITY MODEL

In the probability model, the weights are treated as probabilities of relevance given the occurrence of the query terms in the document. For the notion of relevance feedback with these probabilities, one uses the concept of Bayesian probability. Here, one has Pr(event A | fact B) = Pr(fact B | event A) * Pr(event A)/Pr(fact B), with Pr(.) is the probability of the given argument actually occurring.

For the Bayesian updating for relevance feedback, mathematically one has
$$q'(j) = [(r_j/(r- r_j))] / [(n_j-r_j)/\{(n- n_j)-(r - r_j)\}],$$
q' is the modified query weight for term j, n is the number of retrieved documents, r is the number of documents deemed relevant that were retrieved, nj is the number of retrieved documents that have term j in them, and rj is the number of documents deemed relevant that have term j in them and that were retrieved.

4.5 RELEVANCE FEEDBACK WITH THE BOOLEAN AND FUZZY BOOLEAN MODELS

For the Boolean model without weights or with the fuzzy Boolean model with weights, we cannot provide a simple formula to update the query weights. Thus, we are left with other options.

First of all, we can use common sense. For example, to increase recall, one could use the OR operator to add additional query terms. One could also use more general terms, e.g., dog versus golden retriever. One could also search the entire document rather than just one part (e.g., the keywords, title, or abstract). Moreover, one could use truncation (sometimes called wild card truncation), so that work* could stand for work, worker, workers, works, working, workings, and so forth. On the other hand, to increase precision, one could use the AND operator to demand that documents have both terms within them. One could use more specific terms (e.g., laptop versus computer) or just search specific fields within the document, as mentioned above. One could also use proximity operator to demand that one term occur close to another term, e.g., "information" occurring within two words of "retrieval." Moreover, one could use delimiters to further identify relevant documents, e.g., language being English) or date being no later than 2010.

However, one could also try to compute better queries, with or without weights. One could attempt to search the entire set of all possible queries, which is related to the very difficult theoretical problem in computer science of the satisfiability problem. To do this, there are a variety of techniques, such as linear search (just start searching all of them). There is also the issue of discrete optimization, including tabu search and simulated annealing. We have looked at another alternative.

4.5.1 GENETIC ALGORITHMS (PROGRAMMING) FOR BOOLEAN RELEVANCE FEEDBACK

We have experimented with the idea of using evolutionary computing, specifically, genetic algorithms (GAs), to try to find an improved query based on relevance feedback for a Boolean query, whether weighted or not. The idea is to generate an initial population of queries, perhaps using the original query, the individual terms in the query in simple Boolean expressions, and such. The major issue was the representation of the queries for use in the GA. It was decided to use parse trees where the query is parsed. As an example, consider Figure 4.1 for the rather complex query, "(Dog AND (Cat OR Kitten)) AND (Hamster OR Mouse)."

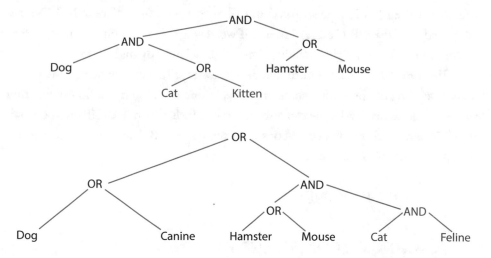

Figure 4.1: Parse Trees for Q1: Query "[Dog AND (Cat OR Kitten)] AND (Hamster OR Mouse)" and Query Q2: "(Dog OR Canine) OR [(Hamster OR Mouse) AND (Cat AND Feline)]."

Queries represented by parse trees can now be stored and manipulated via computerized genetic algorithms.

Now, one should evaluate each member of the current population via a fitness function. We used a combination of recall (Re) and precision (Pn) for then retrieved items evaluated for relevance based on the formula $\alpha Re + (1-\alpha)Pn$, for a parameter $\alpha \varepsilon [0,1]$ as the fitness function. The fitness function determines which members of the current population can continue to be in the population and perhaps to generate further solutions. Then, we consider the best queries in the current population, as determined by the fitness function.

We now randomly pick pairs of queries from the set of best queries and generate new queries via exchanging subtrees; this process is known as crossover. As an example, consider query$_1$: "[Dog AND (Cat OR Kitten)] AND (Hamster OR Mouse)" and query$_2$: "(Dog OR Canine) OR [(Hamster OR Mouse) AND (Cat AND Feline)]". Exchanging subtrees via crossover yields query$_3$: "[Dog AND (Cat AND Feline)] AND (Hamster OR Mouse)" and query$_4$: "(Dog OR Canine) OR [(Hamster OR Mouse) AND (Cat OR Kitten)]. Note that queries in the current population that are not considered best vis-à-vis the fitness function are dropped from the population.

It is also possible to modify some of the queries in the population via mutation based on a given small probability p. One could negate terms (e.g., "NOT Kitten" instead of "Kitten") or change an AND to OR or vice versa (e.g., "Dog AND Canine" as opposed to "Dog OR Canine)." Again, if weights are involved on the query terms, one could modify the weights, making them slightly larger or slightly smaller.

This process is repeated until one desires to stop. This can be due to the fitness function leveling off, becoming stable in value, or one can stop if the fitness function reaches a satisfactory level. One can also stop if one feels that one has iterated enough times. Once a small set of good queries has been generated, one can use them to retrieve more relevant documents.

4.6 QUERY EXPANSION

4.6.1 ADDING OR CHANGING TERMS

In addition to the concept of relevance feedback, there are other means of modifying the query in order to improve retrieval performance, i.e., recall and precision. Recall the discussion in the previous chapter of the use of common sense. To increase recall, one could use the OR operator to add additional query terms or one could use more general terms, e.g., dog versus golden retriever. On the other hand, to increase precision, one could use the AND operator to demand that documents have all query terms within them or use more specific terms, e.g., laptop versus computer.

Another mechanism is to add related terms to the query, with either an AND or an OR operator, in order to improve retrieval. There has been work on fuzzy thesauri (Miyamoto, 1990) to deal with related terms. Let us consider the use of a controlled vocabulary with a fixed set of terms and defined relationships. A big issue in retrieval research has been to the mapping of terms to concepts.

We have considered (Srinivasan et al., 2001) the Unified Medical Language System (UMLS), generated at the National Library of Medicine for medical literature. The term relationships, alongside an example for the term "1,2-dipalmitoylphosphati-dycholine," are listed below in Table 4.1.

Table 4.1: Term relationships

Relationship	Example
R1 – Synonym	Dipalmitoyllecithin
R2 – Ancestor terms	phosphatidic acids; phospholipids
R3 – Parent term	dimyristoylphosphatidylcholine
R4 – Sibling term	phosphatidycholines
R5 - Qualifier terms	administration and dosage; adverse effects; analogs and derivatives
R6 – Narrower term	colfosceril palmitate
R7 – Related terms	dipalmitoylphosphatidyl; mass concentration; point in time; serum; quantitative
R8 – Co-occuring terms	acetephenones; acids; alcohols; laurates

Note that a parent term implies an immediately broader term, i.e., the original term in question is a special case of the parent term. A sibling term is a term that has the same parent term as the original term. A narrower term implies that it has the original term in question is its parent term. An ancestor term implies that the original term in question is part of a broader set of terms, e.g., a dog is a canine which is in turn a mammal, so that "mammal" is an ancestor term for the original term "dog." Co-occuring terms imply that these terms occur along with the original term in question in several documents. Qualifying terms imply terms that help to explain the concept(s) represented by the original term in question. Finally, related terms are terms that seem to be related to the original term in question but not in a way as specified by the other term relationships.

4.7   FUZZY AND ROUGH SETS FOR DATA MINING OF A CONTROLLED VOCABULARY

Let us focus on the relationship of synonymy. This is because of the fact that this relationship is a partition-type, which has good mathematical properties. Later, we consider other relationships. In order to be a partition, we need first U, a universe of objects, e.g., a set of terms from a controlled vocabulary. Then, we need to subdivide those objects into a series of subsets. To be a partition (also called a foreset), we need this subdivision, labeled R, to be a reflexive, symmetric, and transitive relationship (also called a serial or Euclidean relationship). We can use the notation xRy to state that x is related to y where x and y are elements of U. Moreover, we can use the notation U/R to indicate the set of the partition cells, also called equivalence classes, denoted as $\{C_1, C_2, \ldots, C_n\}$, where n is the number of such partition cells. Note that each partition cell is a subset of U.

Reflexivity requires that x, an element of U, is related to x, e.g., term x is synonymous with itself. Second, symmetry requires that if x and y are elements of U, x is related to y and y is related to x, i.e., if term x is a synonym of term y then term y is a synonym of term x. Finally, transitivity requires that if x, y, and z are elements of U, if x is related to y and y is related to z, then x is related to z; e.g., if term x is a synonym of term y and term y is a synonym of term z, then term x is a synonym of term z. Thus, if U is a set of terms in a controlled vocabulary and R is the relationship of synonymy, each term in a given partition cell Ci is a synonym to each of the other terms in that partition cell.

Now, a rough set S consists of two approximations of the partition relationship R within the universe U. First, we have the lower bound approximation, i.e., the set of partition cell elements where every element of each partition cell is in S. This is represented as

$$apr_R(S) = \{x \in C_i \mid C_i \subseteq S\}.$$

Note that aprR(S) can be interpreted as meaning that each element in S is "very S." Second, we have the upper bound approximation, i.e., the set of partition cell elements where at least one element of each partition cell is in S. This is represented as

$$apr_R(S) = \{x \in C_i \mid C_i \cap S \neq \varphi\}.$$

Note that $apr_R(S)$ can be interpreted as meaning that each element in S is "more or less S."

One can ask how all of this can relate to information retrieval. Let us consider a document D as a collection of terms from the universe U. Let us also consider a query Q as a collection of terms from U. Let us also have the synonymy relationship R as a partition of U. Now, we can use the rough set mechanism to define the similarities of the document D and the query Q. Based on the lower bound approximations of the document D and the query Q, we have

$$\underline{Sim}_R(D,Q) = 1 - |\ \underline{apr}_R(Q) - \underline{apr}_R(Q) \cap \underline{apr}_R(D)|\ /\ |\underline{apr}_R(Q)|.$$

Based on the upper bound approximations of the document D and the query Q, we have

$$Sim_R(D,Q) = 1 - |\ apr_R(Q) - apr_R(Q) \cap apr_R(D)|\ /\ |apr_R(Q)|.$$

Note that $|.|$ indicates the cardinality of the set that is the argument of the function, i.e., the number of elements in the set.

4.7.1   FUZZY SET NOTATION FOR ROUGH SETS

All this is reasonable for situations where the synonymy relationship is well defined as is the document and query. However, as we have seen, the query and the document definitions can be imprecise or fuzzy. Moreover, the notion of synonymy, on which the partition R is defined, can be imprecise or fuzzy.

For the lower bound approximation of the set S, given the universe U and the partition relationship R, we have the membership function $\mu apr(R(S)(x)$ as

$$\mu_{\underline{apr}(R(S))}(x) = \inf\{\mu_S(y) \mid y \in U, xRy\} = \inf\{1 - \mu_R(x,y) \mid y \notin S\} = \inf\{\max[\mu_S(y), 1 - \mu_R(x,y) \mid y \in U\},$$

for $x \varepsilon U$. Note that inf stands for the infimum function, i.e., the greatest element (although not necessarily in the set) that is less than or equal to all elements of the set. It is also called the greatest lower bound (GLB) of the set. Of course, max(.), shorthand for maximum, is the function yielding the largest element within the set of elements in the argument of the max function.

For the upper bound approximation of the set S, given the universe U and the partition relationship R, we have the membership function $\mu_{apr(R(S)}(x)$ as

$$\mu_{apr(R(S)}(x) = \sup\{\mu_S(y) \mid y \in U, xRy\} = \sup\{\mu_R(x,y) \mid y \in S\} = \sup\{\min[\mu_S(y), \mu_R(x,y) \mid y \in U\},$$

for $x \varepsilon U$. Note that sup stands for the supremum function, i.e., the smallest element (although not necessarily in the set) that is greater than or equal to all elements of the set. It is also called the least upper bound (LUB) of the set. Of course, min(.), shorthand for minimum, is the function yielding the smallest element within the set of elements in the argument of the min function.

For the similarity functions, one uses the summation of the appropriate membership functions, which are the μ functions for the cardinality functions in the similarity formulae above.

4.8 EXTENSIONS OF THE ROUGH SET APPROACH TO RETRIEVAL

4.8.1 ROUGH FUZZY SETS

Suppose that one assumes that the synonymy relationship is crisp, or not fuzzy. That is, terms are either totally synonymous or they are not. However, the representations of the documents and the query are fuzzy, i.e., there are term weights that help describe the contents of the documents and the query.

Here, one can use an alpha (α) cutoff. This implies that one can revise the membership functions so that $\mu_{apr(R(S))}(x)$ can be set to 1 if $\mu_{apr(R(S))}(x) \geq \alpha$, otherwise, it is set to 0. This is also the case for $\mu_{apr(R(S))}(x)$.

4.8.2 FUZZY ROUGH SETS

We can also consider a scenario if one assumes that the representations of the documents and the query are crisp, i.e., not fuzzy. That is, the terms assigned to the documents are present or they are not, as the case for the query. However, the synonymy relationship is fuzzy. That is, the terms' synonymy relationships are weighted, i.e., there are term weights that help describe the extent to which terms are synonyms. Again, alpha cutoffs could be applied.

4.8.3 GENERALIZED FUZZY AND ROUGH SETS

Again, if one assumes the most general case where the representations of the documents and the query, as well as the synonymy relationship are all fuzzy, then, one uses the membership functions as defined above.

4.8.4 NONEQUIVALENCE RELATIONSHIPS

We have generated a model for the synonymy relationship which is a true partition relationship. However, we can ponder what if one has one of the other term relationships, which do not have all the properties required for a true partition. For example, consider the parent relationship, with is neither reflexive nor symmetric. A specific example can show this; a dog is a canine but not all canines are dogs. Thus, the term "canine" is a parent term for the term "dog" but the reverse is not true. Moreover, the term "dog" is not a parent term for "dog." Thus, this notion of a term hierarchy is a weak ordering of the terms in the universe. For such hierarchy relationships, i.e., the ancestor or parent or narrower term relationships, we have

$$\text{apr}_R(S)=\{x\in U \mid R(x)\subseteq S\} \text{ and } \text{apr}_R(S)=\{x\in U \mid R(x)\cap S \neq \varphi\}\,,$$

where $R(x)$ are the set of terms related to term x.

To be more specific here, for a given limit n, we could have

$$\text{apr}_R(S)=\{x\in U \mid |R(x)| - |R(x)\cap S| \leq n\} \text{ and } \text{apr}_R(S)=\{x\in U \mid |R(x)\cap S| \geq n \}.$$

Note that previously we assumed that $n = 0$. Or, for a given parameter $\gamma\in[0,1]$, we could have

$$\text{apr}_R(S)=\{x\in U \mid |R(x)\cap S| / |R(x)| \geq 1-\gamma\} \text{ and } \text{apr}_R(S)=\{x\in U \mid |R(x)\cap S| / |R(x)| \geq \gamma \}/.$$

4.8.5 COMBINING SEVERAL RELATIONSHIPS SIMULTANEOUSLY

We have seen that there are different term relationships that can co-occur. For example, the terms "dog" and "pooch" might be synonyms while we have seen that "dog" and "canine" have a parental relationship. Thus, we want to be able to combine several relationships simultaneously.

Using the fuzzy AND and OR for intersection and union, respectively, of lower and upper bounds, for two relationships R_i and R_j, we have

$$\text{apr}_{R_i \text{ AND } R_j}(D) = \text{apr}_{R_i}(D) \cap \text{apr}_{R_j}(D), \quad \text{apr}_{R_i \text{ AND } R_j}(Q) = \text{apr}_{R_i}(Q) \cap \text{apr}_{R_j}(Q),$$
$$\text{apr}_{R_i \text{ AND } R_j}(D) = \text{apr}_{R_i}(D) \cap \text{apr}_{R_j}(D), \quad \text{apr}_{R_i \text{ AND } R_j}(Q) = \text{apr}_{R_i}(Q) \cap \text{apr}_{R_j}(Q);$$

and

$$\text{apr}_{R_i \text{ OR } R_j}(D) = \text{apr}_{R_i}(D) \cup \text{apr}_{R_j}(D) \qquad \text{apr}_{R_i \text{ OR } R_j}(Q) = \text{apr}_{R_i}(Q) \cup \text{apr}_{R_j}(Q)$$
$$\text{apr}_{R_i \text{ OR } R_j}(D) = \text{apr}_{R_i}(D) \cup \text{apr}_{R_j}(D) \qquad \text{apr}_{R_i \text{ OR } R_j}(Q) = \text{apr}_{R_i}(Q) \cup \text{apr}_{R_j}(Q).$$

Thus, one can combine term relationships via the AND or the OR operator as desired.

CHAPTER 5

Clustering for Retrieval

5.1 INTRODUCTION

The concept of clustering can be explained as the gathering together of like objects. For example, one can cluster a group of students by various characteristics, e.g., gender, university major, grade point average, and so forth. In terms of information retrieval, one can cluster documents together based on their similarity to each other.

One can cluster documents on the basis of the terms they contain, perhaps using frequency weights as suggested in Chapter 2. An alternative is to cluster documents based on the co-occurrence of citations (i.e., references) to other documents. Note that it is possible to group small clusters into larger super-clusters. A third, rather interesting, idea is to cluster the terms based on the documents in which they occur. Of course, this does not relate to the aggregation of views used to evaluate the relevance of a document to a query.

5.2 APPLICATIONS

The benefits of clustering lie in the possible applications. One can use clustering of documents in order to categorize those documents by topic. For example, clustering documents allows one to retrieve all documents in a given cluster or hierarchy of clusters. This is the major point of this chapter. However, there are other applications worthy of mention.

If the "documents" are web pages, one can do post-hoc clustering of retrieved web pages. For this last notion, a search for "Yellowstone" yields approximately 100 web pages as a result, with about 60 of them being relevant to the user. Relevant sites have terms as follows: "buffalo," "deer," "wolf," "geyser," "faithful," "spring," "reserve," "lodge," and "bus." Another example is that a search for the term "jaguar" can group pages related to cars, or jungle animals, or even software.

An additional application of clustering is in the area of text mining where one seeks patterns and trends within natural language data. As already noted, a different notion is to cluster terms in order to build a thesaurus of related terms. The concept of a thesaurus allows for query expansion, as noted in Chapter 5.

Finally, one can generate user profiles by clustering of search terms. This can allow for better understanding of user needs and to generate query templates for common queries. Searching for diapers, wipes, and baby strollers would indicate the user is probably a new parent; this would allow a search engine to customize the ads placed on the site to be more parent-centric and user applicable.

Outside of retrieval, one can use clustering for parallel processing, load balancing, and even fault tolerance.

5.3   CLUSTERING ALGORITHMS

One of the algorithmic issues is how to generate the clusters. A major theme is that documents within a given cluster should be more similar to each other than to documents in different clusters. One can start by considering each document as an individual cluster and then start to group them into small clusters then into larger clusters, i.e., a bottom-up methodology. Note that clusters C_r and C_s are merged into one super cluster C_t if the similarity of the clusters two original small clusters is maximal. Note that cluster similarity implies a similarity between the two smaller clusters' centroids, where a centroid is an average of the document vectors taken over all documents in the cluster.

On the other hand, one can start by having each document grouped into one super cluster, then breaking them into smaller and smaller clusters, i.e., a top-down methodology.

Some of the various algorithms include connectivity-based or hierarchical clustering, based on the idea of documents being more related to nearby documents than to documents farther away. These algorithms connect documents to form clusters based on their distance. A cluster can be described largely by the maximum distance needed to connect parts of the cluster.

As an alternative, in centroid-based or k-means clustering, clusters are represented by a central vector, which may not necessarily be a member of any actual document.

Distribution-based clustering is most closely related to statistics where clusters can then easily be defined as documents belonging most likely to the same distribution. A convenient property of this approach is that this closely resembles the way artificial data sets are generated: by sampling random objects from a distribution.

In density-based clustering, the clusters are defined as areas of higher density than the remainder of the documents. Documents in these sparse areas, that are required to separate clusters, are usually considered to be noise and border points.

One of the issues is whether or not one needs to specify in advance how many clusters are to be created. Another issue is how many passes through the data are required to create these clusters.

5.4 SIMILARITY MEASURES

Another issue is how to determine the document similarities. For our purpose here, let us assume that each document can be represented as a vector of term weights, i.e., document $d_i = \{t_{ij}\}$, where t_{ij} is the weight of term j on document i. These weights may be calculated as the tdf-if weights, as discussed in Chapter 3. The most common similarity measures include the following:

- Inner Product (IP): $Sim(d_i,d_k) = \Sigma_j t_{ij}{}^* t_{kj}$ (a measure of overlap)

- Jacuard Coefficient: $Sim(d_i,d_k) = \Sigma_j t_{ij}{}^* t_{kj} / [\Sigma_j t_{ij}{}^* t_{ij} + \Sigma_j t_{kj}{}^* t_{kj} - \Sigma_j t_{ij}{}^* t_{kj}]$

- Dice Coefficient: $Sim(di,dk) = 2^* \Sigma_j t_{ij}{}^* t_{kj} / [\Sigma_j t_{ij}{}^* t_{ij}{}^* \Sigma_j t_{kj}{}^* t_{kj}]$

- Cosine Coefficient: $\Sigma_j t_{ij}{}^* t_{kj} \sqrt{[\Sigma_j t_{ij}{}^* t_{ij}{}^* \Sigma_j t_{kj}{}^* t_{kj}]}$ (normalized length)

The most common of these is the cosine coefficient.

5.5 FUZZY CLUSTERING

Fuzzy clustering techniques exist where each document can be placed within several clusters, with a given strength of belonging to each cluster. As noted, this notion can be used to expand the set of the documents retrieved in response to a query. Documents associated with retrieved documents, i.e., in the same cluster, can be retrieved. The degree of association of a document with the retrieved documents does influence its retrieval status value and therefore its rank in the list of retrieved results.

5.6 THE FUZZY C-MEANS ALGORITHM

This is both a hierarchical- and a centroid-based algorithm, and is based on a bottom-up approach. First, one must specify the parameter c, the number of clusters to be generated. Then, one has the optimization problem of minimizing the function:

$$J = \Sigma_{k=1} \Sigma_{i=1} (\mu_{ki})^m ||p_i - v_k||^2,$$

where m is a parameter > 1 and n is the number of documents to be clustered. This optimization is subject to the constraints:

$$\Sigma_{k=1} \mu_{ki} = 1 \text{ for } i=1,2,\ldots,n \text{ and}$$
$$\mu_{ki} \geq 0 \text{ for } i=1,2,\ldots,n \text{ and } k=1,2,\ldots,c .$$

Note that μ_{ki} = the degree or weight of membership of document i in cluster k, p_i = the term weight vector for document I, and v_k = the centroid for cluster k (i.e., the average of the document vectors taken over all documents in cluster k).

The solution must be calculated iteratively and is given by

$$\mu_{ki} = [||\ p_i - v_k||^2]^{-1/(m-1)}/ \Sigma_{j=1}[||\ p_i - v_j||^2]^{-1/(m-1)}$$
$$v_k = \Sigma_{i=1}\ (\mu_{ki})^m p_i / \Sigma_{i=1}\ (\mu_{ki})^m$$

5.7 A TESTING EXAMPLE

To try out these clustering methodologies, a test was conducted. The data were found in the "Engineering Design Compendium" (EDC), an anthology of ergonomic research conducted at the Wright-Patterson Air Force Base. More specifically, the Audiology section of the EDC was used (Kraft et al., 2000; Chen et al., 2000).

First, there was some preprocessing of the data. In order to reduce the dimension of the 114 document vectors from 2,857 keywords, a selection of the top 100 maximal-weighted keywords was made. Note that the maximal weight t_j of term j is $max_i\ t_{ij}$. Thus, we selected the top 100 keywords when sorted in descending order of t_j.

The result, using fuzzy clustering via the fuzzy C-means algorithm with experimentally determined m= 1.1 and then m = 1.4, yielded 12 clusters. While not usual, this was compared to regular clustering, and unexpectedly showed a small improvement over the fuzzy clusters. Moreover, the results were compared to the clusters generated manually be the subject experts, and the computer-generated clusters were good according to those experts, albeit that the computer-generated clusters were not all that different from the manual ones.

One issue was that clusters are generally seen as symmetric, i.e., document d_i's similarity to document d_j is the same as the similarity of d_j to d_i. One notes that links via the see-also mechanism in EDDC were not necessarily symmetric.

5.7.1 FUZZY RULE DISCOVERY

Clustering of documents can offer a different view of dealing with term weights, especially in terms of query expansion. Consider documents in a cluster and look at the term weights in the centroid of that cluster. Now, one can generate rules on the order of "the weight of term j exceeding a threshold w implies that term k must exceed a threshold w'," i.e., r: $(t_j \geq w) \rightarrow (t_k \geq w')$ for terms in documents in the same cluster. Then, one can use these rules to expand the query by adding additional terms with weights to increase performance (i.e., precision).

The algorithm for doing this is as follows.

- Normalize cluster centroid v_k.

- Sort the terms in descending order of weights in the cluster and consider the first $N \geq 2$ terms.

- Build term pairs from the chosen terms in each cluster center in the form of $<[t_j, w], [t_k, w']>$.

- Merge multiple occurrence of the same pairs with different weights (use minimums).

- Build two rules from each pair above: $[t_j \geq w] \rightarrow [t_k \geq w']$ and $[t_k \geq w'] \rightarrow [t_j \geq w]$.

- Use these rules to modify a query q: q' = q with weight for term k modified to be w' if weight of term k < w' but weight of term j ≥ w.

- Repeatedly apply fuzzy rules until no more applicable rules can be found.

Note that the final modified query is independent of the order of rule applications.

As an example from the EDC Audiology data, assume a query q = <"pitch", 0.8> and <"adapt",0.4>. After modification via the fuzzy rule discovery method, the new query , q' = <"pitch",0.8> and <"adapt",0.4> and <"interrupt", 0.2029>, and <"modulate", 0.2399> and <"tone", 0.6155>. Note that q' gives improved precision over q.

CHAPTER 6

Uses of Information Retrieval Today

This book has covered a wide range of topics from the beginning need of information storage to the need of that information to be searchable. Times have changed from using paper decimal systems in libraries to computer databases to cloud based web pages that are on multiple servers. The need for relevant information remains the same no matter the domain.

Chapter 1 introduced the notion of information retrieval, offering definitions of IR and of the important concept of relevance. In addition, it offered both a brief historical view of IR and some modern areas of research, especially where fuzzy modeling has the potential to offer some interesting insights. Applications of IR to modern computing problems were mentioned, as well as where fuzziness occurs in IR.

Chapter 2 introduced the notion of IR modeling. This included the traditional models, Boolean, probability, and vector space, as well as some modern concepts. It also developed some fuzzy set theory models for IR. Chapter 2 also presented a clear comparison of the Boolean models to the fuzzy models where it can clearly be seen the strengths and weaknesses in both models and where and why both models would be more useful over another.

Some techniques for searching the data has been discussed as well as how to determine if data is similar when searching. Chapter 3 talks about how to put weights on specific data to give certain data more precedence when searching and some common comparison calculations that are used to measure how well a match is detected. When someone is not interested in either a yes or no match, the fuzzy measure can be introduced, these measures or weights can determine how much how close a match is based on a degree of membership. This method of weighting a search or weighting a search term is the defining feature that separates the fuzzy from non-fuzzy searches, it also can be modified to alter the degree of match in a search. The weights in a search play a very important part as is demonstrated in future chapters.

This introduction of fuzzy membership has now allowed IRS to return a broader list of matches to the user, instead of basing a match on matching or not, yes or no. Using this membership function and the new fuzzy algorithms, searches like Google can now search based on a word or combination of words that will give the user a better chance of finding what they are looking for.

Other advancements like relevance feedback allow users to redefine a search based on the results over and over until a desired list of results or until the exact match is found. Once a list of results is presented, using algorithms presented in Chapter 4, the user can use the results that they deem a match to help the search better refine the corpus they are using and eventually find the perfect result.

Chapter 5 presented an overview of the concept of clustering. Clustering is another concept that allows searches to group like terms together to help hone in on that perfect match to a user's query. Many applications are using this approach. Things such as neural nets, and grid computing make sense to use a clustered-based IR system. Because clusters can be added and deleted as needed, when computing in a grid computing system, like Beowulf Clusters, the nodes can be added on the network and added to the IR system and immediately searched as needed.

Other exciting uses for IRS include the most common web search: Google. We have all searched the internet for something we are looking for and received a list of matched items. What Google is doing with that search, along with the other information they can gather, like the geographic information about your computer, and your search history. They are using that information to filter the ads that appear on the side on the web page. That allows users to have a more personalized web browsing experience and allows ads and companies to be seen more often. If a company that a user would never shop from places an ad on a page, that is wasted space, versus utilizing all the free space on a page with subliminal ads that will appeal to the user. It would be like shopping with blinders on where items that don't apply to you get filtered out and only items that you have purchased or would may purchase in the future are visible.

Other common searches include the National Library of Medicine as mentioned in Chapter 4, and even the digital library of dissertations and theses that helps colleges and universities determine if a topic has been covered or not. Other digital libraries include the ETANA Archaeological Digital Library, the National Science Digital Library, and many more.

Other interesting applications that include information retrieval include Google maps, GARMIN Software, Yahoo!, Firefox, NASA, MapQuest, Apple, Siri, and man many others. If there is information that is needed there is probably an information retrieval application needed. Moreover, we have seen that the use of fuzzy set theory can potentially be of some use for both researchers and practitioners.

Bibliography

Alonso, O., Hearst, M.A., and Kamps, J. (2015). Overview of Graph Search and Beyond. *GSB '15*, 1. 10, 11

Baeza-Yates, R. and Ribeiro-Neto, B. (2011). *Modern Information Retrieval the Concepts and Technology behind Search*. 2nd edition. Addison Wesley:Harlow, UK. 1, 15, 17, 19, 20, 31

Barry, C.L. (1994). User-defined relevance criteria: An exploratory study. *Journal of the American Society for Information Science*, 45(3), 149–159. DOI: /10.1002/(SICI)1097-4571(199404)45:3<149::AID-ASI5>3.0.CO;2-J. 8

Bast, H., Buchhold, B., and Haussmann, E. (2015). Relevance scores for triples from type-like relations. Presented at *SIGIR 2015*, ACM, Santiago, Chili. DOI: 10.1145/2766462.2767734. 13

Belkin, N. J. and Croft, W.B. (1992). Information filtering and information retrieval: two sides of the same coin? *Communications of the ACM*, 35(12), 29–38. DOI: 10.1145/138859.138861. 15

Bookstein, A. (1980). Fuzzy requests: an approach to weighted Boolean searches. *Journal of the American Society for Information Science*, 31(4), 240–247. DOI: 10.1002/asi.4630310403. 17

Bordogna, G., Carrara, G., and Pasi, G. (1992). Extending Boolean information retrieval: A fuzzy model based on linguistic variables. In *Fuzzy Systems, 1992 IEEE International Conference on*, pp. 769–776. DOI: 10.1109/FUZZY.1992.258753. 17

Bordogna, G., Pasi, G., and Yager, R. (2003). Soft approaches to distributed information retrieval. *International Journal of Approximate Reasoning* 34(2–3), 105–120. DOI: 10.1016/j.ijar.2003.07.003. 22

Bordogna, G. and Pasi, G., (2005). Personalised indexing and retrieval of heterogeneous structured documents. *Information Retrieval*, 8(2), 301–318. DOI: 10.1007/s10791-005-5664-x. 32

Bordogna, G. and Pasi, G., (2001). A user-adaptive indexing model of structured documents. Fuzzy systems. *The 10th IEEE International Conference on Fuzzy Systems 2001*, v. 2, pp. 984–989. DOI: 10.1109/fuzz.2001.1009124. 32

Bordogna, G. and Pasi, G. (1995). Controlling retrieval through a user-adaptive representation of documents. *International Journal of Approximate Reasoning* 12(3–4), April–May 1995, pp. 317–339. DOI: 10.1016/0888-613x(94)00036-3. 32

Bordogna, G. and Pasi, G. (1993). A fuzzy linguistic approach generalizing Boolean information retrieval: A model and its evaluation. *Journal of the American Society for information Science*, 44(2), 70–82. DOI: 10.1002/(SICI)1097-4571(199303)44:2<70::AID-ASI2>3.0.CO;2-I. 17, 26

Bradley, R.A. and Terry, M.E. (1952). Rank analysis of incomplete block designs, I. The method of paired comparisons. *Biometrika*, 39, 324–345. DOI: 10.2307/2334029. 23

Buell, D.A. and Kraft, D.H. (1981a). Performance measurement in a fuzzy retrieval environment. In *Proceedings of the Fourth International Conference on Information Storage and Retrieval*, Oakland, CA; ACM/SIGIR Forum, 16(1), May 31– June 2, pp. 56–62. DOI: 10.1145/511754.511762.

Buell, D.A. and Kraft, D.H. (1981b). A model for a weighted retrieval system. *Journal of the American Society for Information Science*, 32(3), 211–216. DOI: 10.1002/asi.4630320307.

Buell, D.A and Kraft, D.H. (1981c). Threshold values and Boolean retrieval systems. *Information Processing and Management*, 17, 127–136. DOI: 10.1016/S0306-4573(81)80004-0.

Cater, S.C. and Kraft, D.H. (1989). A generalization and clarification of the Waller-Kraft wish-list, *Information Processing and Management*, 25, 15–25. DOI: 10.1016/0306-4573(89)90088-5.

Cater, S.C. and Kraft, D.H. (1987). TIRS: A topological information retrieval system satisfying the requirements of the Waller-Kraft wish list. In *Proceedings of the tenth annual ACM/SIGIR International Conference on Research and Development in Information Retrieval*, New Orleans, LA, June, 1987, pp. 171–180. DOI: 10.1145/42005.42025.

Chen, G. and Pham, T.T. (2001). *Introduction to Fuzzy Sets, Fuzzy Logic, and Fuzzy Control Systems*. CRC Press:Boca Raton, FL.

Chen, J., Mikulcic, A., and Kraft, D.H. (2000). "An integrated approach to information retrieval with fuzzy clustering and fuzzy inferencing," in Pons, O., Vila, M.A., and Kacprzyk, J. (eds.), *Knowledge Management in Fuzzy Databases*, Physica-Verlag:Heidelberg, Germany. DOI: 10.1007/978-3-7908-1865-9_15. 52

Chen, S.-T., Yu, T.-J., Chen, L.-C., and Liu, F.-P. (2016). A Novel User Profile Learning Approach with Fuzzy Constraint for News Retrieval, *International Journal of Intelligent System*, 32, 249–265. DOI: 10.1002/int.21840.

Chen, X., Bennett, P.N., Collins-Thompson, K., and Horvitz, E. (2013, February). Pairwise ranking aggregation in a crowdsourced setting. *Proceedings of the Sixth ACM International Conference on Web Search and Data Mining* ACM, pp. 193–202. DOI: 10.1145/2433396.2433420. 23

Colvin, E. (2014). Using fuzzy sets for retrieval of software for reuse. Dissertation, Colorado Technical University, Colorado Springs, CO. 4, 10

Croft, W.B., Metzler, D., and Strohman, T. (2010). *Search Engines: Information Retrieval in Practice*. Addison-Wesley: Boston, MA. 21

Cruz, N.P., Taboada, M., and Mitkov, R. (2016). A machine-learning approach to negation and speculation detection for sentiment analysis. *Journal of the Association for Information Science and Technology*, 67(9), 2118–2136. DOI: 10.1002/asi.23533.

da Costa Pereira, C., Dragoni, M., and Pasi, G. (2009). Multidimensional relevance: A new aggregation criterion. LNCS v. 5478, Advances in Information Retrieval, In *Proceedings of the BCS -IRSG European Conference on Information Retrieval, ECIR 2009*, Toulouse, France, 2009, pp. 264–275. DOI: 10.1007/978-3-642-00958-7_25. 22

Damiani, E., Marrara, S., Pasi, G. (2008), A flexible extension of XPath to improve XML querying, In *Proceedings of ACM/SIGIR, 200*. 22

Diaz, E.D., De, A., and Raghavan, V. (2005). A comprehensive OWA-based framework for result merging in metasearch. In *Rough Sets, Fuzzy Sets, Data Mining, and Granular Computing*. Springer:Berlin Heidelberg, pp. 193–201. DOI: 10.1007/11548706_21. 23

dtSearch (2016). dtSearch How it works. Retrieved from https://www.dtsearch.com/.

Dupret, G. (2011, January). Discounted cumulative gain and user decision models. In *String Processing and Information Retrieval.* Springer:Berlin Heidelberg, pp. 2–13. DOI: 10.1007/978-3-642-24583-1_2. 29

Fox, E.A. and Sharan, S. (1986). A comparison of two methods for soft Boolean operator interpretation in information retrieval. Technical Report, Virginia Polytechnic Institute and State University, Blacksburg, VA. 17

Frakes, W.B. and Baeza-Yates, R. (1992). *Information Retrieval Data Structures and Algorithms.* Prentice Hall: Englewood Cliffs, NJ. 20, 26, 27, 33

Ghorab, R., Zhou, D., O'Connor, A, and Wade, V. (2013). Personalised information retrieval: survey and classification. *User Modeling and User-Adapted Interaction.* 23(4), 381–443. DOI: 10.1007/s11257-012-9124-1. 10

Gupta, Y., Saini, A., and Saxena, A.K. (2015). A new fuzzy logic based ranking Function for efficient IR system. *Expert Systems with Applications*, 42(3), pp. 1223–1234. DOI: 10.1016/j.eswa.2014.09.009.

Herrera-Viedma, E. and Pasi, G. (2006). Soft approaches to information retrieval and information access on the Web: An introduction to the special topic section. *Journal of the American Society for Information Science and Technology.* (2/15/2006). DOI: 10.1002/asi.20305. 22

Kraft, D.H. (1985). Advances in information retrieval: Where is that /#*%@^ record? In *Advances in Computers*, Yovits, M., ed., 24. Academic Press:New York, pp. 277–318. 5, 7

Kraft D., Bordogna G., and Pasi, G. (1999). Fuzzy set techniques. In *Information Retrieval, in "Fuzzy Sets in Approximate Reasoning and Information Systems"*, J. C. Bezdek, D. Dubois and H. Prade (eds.), The Handbooks of Fuzzy Sets Series, Kluwer Academic Publishers, pp. 469–510.

Kraft, D.H., Bordogna, G., and Pasi, G. (1995). An extended fuzzy linguistic approach to generalize Boolean information retrieval, *Journal of Information Sciences, Applications*, 2(3), 119–134.

Kraft, D., Bordogna, G., and Pasi, G. (1998) Information retrieval systems: Where is the fuzz? In *Fuzzy Systems Proceedings, 1998. IEEE World Congress on Computational Intelligence.* The 1998 IEEE International Conference on, 2, 1367–1372. DOI: 10.1109/FUZZY.1998.686318. 12, 15

Kraft, D.H., Chen, J., and Mikulcic, A. (2000). Combining fuzzy clustering and fuzzy inferencing in information retrieval, *FUZZ-IEEE 2000*, San Antonio, TX. 52

Marrara, S., Panzeri, E., and Pasi, G (2011). An analysis of efficient data structures for evaluating flexible constraints on XML documents. *Flexible Query Answering Systems - 9th International Conference, FQAS. 2011*, Ghent, Belgium, 2011. LNCS vol. 7022. Springer, pp. 294–3052. DOI: 10.1007/978-3-642-24764-4_26. 22

Maarek, Y., Berry, D., and Kaiser, G. (1991). An information retrieval approach for automatically constructing software libraries. *IEEE Transactions on Software Engineering*, 7(8), 800–813. DOI: 10.1109/32.83915. 10

Megter (2016). 5 Excel add ins every data scientist should install. Data Science Central. Retrieved from http://www.datasciencecentral.com/profiles/blogs/5-excel-add- ins-every-data-scientist-should-install.

Minkov, E., Cohen, W.W., and Ng, A.Y. (2006). Contextual search and name disambiguation in email using graphs. In *Proceedings of the 29th Annual International ACM SIGIR Conference on Research and Development in Information Retrieval*, pp. 27–34. DOI: 10.1145/1148170.1148179. 15

Miyamoto, S. (1990). *Fuzzy Sets in Information Retrieval and Cluster Analysis*. Kluwer Academic Publishers:Dordrecht, Netherlands. DOI: 10.1007/978-94-015-7887-5. 43

Park, D., Kim, H., Zhai, C., and Guo, L. (2015). Retrieval of relevant opinion sentences for new products. Presented at *SIGIR 2015* ACM:Santiago, Chili. 11

Pereira, C., Dragoni, M., and Pasi, G. (2012). Multidimensional relevance: Prioritized aggregation in a personalized information retrieval setting. *Information Processing and Management*, 48(2). 26

Robertson, S., Zaragoza, H., and Taylor, M. (2004). Simple BM25 extension to multiple weighted fields. *ACM Conference on Information Knowledge 2004*, November, 8–13. DOI: 10.1145/1031171.1031181. 21

Salton, G., Fox, E., and Wu, H. (1983). Extended Boolean information retrieval. *Communications of the ACM*. 26(12), 1022–1036. DOI: 10.1145/182.358466. 1, 34

Srinivasan, P., Ruiz, M. E., Kraft, D. H., and Chen, J. (2001). Vocabulary mining for information retrieval: rough sets and fuzzy sets. *Information Processing & Management*, 37(1), 15-38. DOI: 10.1016/S0306-4573(00)00014-5. 43

Tamine-Lechani, L., Boughanem, M., and Daoud, M. (2010). Evaluation of contextual information retrieval effectiveness: overview of issues and research. *Knowledge and Information Systems*, 24(1), 1–34. DOI: 10.1007/s10115-009-0231-1. 15

Tamir, D.E., Rishe, N.D. and Kandel, A. (2015). *Fifty Years of Fuzzy Logic and its Applications*. Springer:New York. DOI:10.1007/978-3-319-19683-1. 36, 37

Turpin, A. and Scholer, F. (2006). User performance versus precision measures for simple search tasks. In *Proceedings of the 29th Annual International ACM SIGIR Conference on Research and Development in Information Retrieval*, ACM, pp. 11–18. DOI: 10.1145/1148170.1148176. 28

Yager, R. (1988). On ordered weighted averaging aggregation operators in multi-criteria decision making. *IEEE Transactions on Systems Man and Cybernetics*. 18(1), 183–190. DOI: 10.1109/21.87068. 26

Xu, J. and Croft, B. (1996). Query expansion using local and global document analysis. Presented at *SIGIR 1996*, ACM:Zurich, Switzerland. DOI: 10.1145/243199.243202. 21

Waller, W.G. and Kraft, D.H. (1979). A mathematical model of a weighted Boolean retrieval system. *Information Processing and Management*, 15, 235–245. DOI: 10.1016/0306-4573(79)90030-X.

Zadrożny, S. and Nowacka, K. (2009). Fuzzy information retrieval model revisited. *Fuzzy Sets and Systems*, 160(15), 2173–2191. DOI: 10.1016/j.fss.2009.02.012.

Zhao, D. and Strotmann, A. (2016). Dimensions and uncertainties of author citation rankings: Lessons learned from frequency-weighted in-text citation counting. *Journal of the Association for Information Science and Technology*, 67(3), 671-682. DOI: 10.1002/asi.23418. 9

Author Biographies

Donald H. Kraft's degrees are from Purdue University, where he majored in industrial engineering, specializing in operations research. He has taught at Purdue University, the University of Maryland, Indiana University, the University of California—Berkeley, the University of California—Los Angeles, the U.S. Air Force Academy, and Louisiana State University—where he served as chair and is now a professor emeritus. He is currently an adjunct professor at Colorado Technical University. He has been named a Fellow of IEEE, AAAS, and IFSA, as well as an ACM Distinguished Scientist and a LSU Distinguished Professor. He is also a winner of both the ASIST Research Award and Award of Merit. He served for 24 years as Editor of *JASIST* and is a Past President of ASIST. His research interests include information retrieval, fuzzy set theory, genetic algorithms, rough sets, operations research, and information science.

Erin Colvin's degrees are a B.S. in computer science from Middle Tennessee State University; an M.Ed. in secondary education from Chaminade University of Honolulu; an M.S. in computer science from American Sentinel University; and a D.C. S. in computer science from Colorado Technical University. She has worked as a software engineer for Square D Company creating front-end software for electrical metering devices for companies such as BASF, Northrup Grumman, and the University of New Mexico. She has taught at Anne Arundel Community College, Southern New Hampshire University, John Hopkins University Center for Talented Youth and Regis University. Currently, Dr. Colvin is an instructor in the Computer Science Department at Western Washington University. Her research interests include information retrieval, fuzzy set theory, genetic algorithms, and software reuse.

ed in the United States
ker & Taylor Publisher Services